Lost and Found In Translation

Dr. Ibrahim Saad

I

Published by New Generation Publishing in 2012

www.generation-publishing.com

email: ibrahimsaad1948@yahoo.com

 **New Generation Publishing**

Contents

Foreword

The framework for this book is provided by the linguistic description of Patricia L. McEldowney. Her system of textual analysis and her system for the recycling of information from an original input text, through "transition notes" and visual representations, to various levels of spoken and written learner output text, were originally developed as the basis for learning materials and classroom tasks for learners of English as a second and foreign language. A model has been developed for learners of translation whose control of a target language still needed practice.

In this respect, she has kindly given permission for the use in this book of textual materials and self-learning tasks developed while she was lecturing in the School of Education at the University of Manchester.

I am also in her debt for the helpful suggestions she has made during the writing of this book.

Dr Ibrahim Saad.

Preface

Much has been written elsewhere about the theory of translation. The focus here, however, is on a generalised linguistic description as the basis for understanding and learning to translate different types of text. A framework for analysing universal text types is provided through the medium of English. It is then shown how this analysis can be used as the basis for re-building the text in another language, in this case Arabic. Moreover, the analysis reveals core examples of each type of text type identified and shows how more and more sophisticated forms occur within the context of each. This obviously has implications for course design and a general path from core to more sophisticated is exemplified.

It is implicit within this approach that the concern is with understanding and transferring the cohesion and coherence of text. The grammatical framework revealed by the textual analysis provides the context for dealing with discrete lexical items and collocations within. Though the languages exemplified here are English and Arabic it is believed that the process outlined has universal application.

The main focus is on working with factual text types. Such text allows trainee translators to transfer information from one language to another with minimal loss or gain at the same time as they are able to improve their control of the languages involved. This foundation is then shown to be the spring-board for dealing with much more complex, creative text typical of the novel and short story, poetry and drama. By its very nature such text demands a much greater personal response on part of the translator.

The book integrates theory and practice and, where appropriate, uses an interactive style which encourages active learning. Examples used in the explanations are followed by *Try This* tasks. These tasks provide the opportunity for the reader to work through similar examples in order to develop a deeper understanding of the principles being illustrated. To provide immediate feedback solutions are provided in the Key often together with some additional explanation.

Patricia L. McEldowney

Chapter One
Language Variation

1.1   Introduction

The purpose of this chapter is to introduce the idea of language variation as an introduction to how different types of language present different problems for the translator. A central hypothesis is that a piece of literature is a personal production designed to achieve a particular effect or artistic experience. Interacting with such text therefore requires a great deal of personal involvement on the part of the reader or translator. At the other end of the scale, the translation of text which has the purpose of communicating factual information in an impersonal manner involves much less choice on the part of the translator. Learning to translate factual language is an important prerequisite for learning to translate literature.

A sound knowledge of factual language (1.4) can be seen to develop an awareness of a norm from which literary text deviates in order to make a special impact. Further, beginning with more predictable text will enable those who come to translation before they are completely fluent in English, for example, to improve their English reading skills. Such preparation helps translators deal with the greater complexities of literary and other less predictable text. When learning to translate, more predictable text provides a better basis for learning how to improve the quality of the output while at the same time preserving as much as possible of the original information in the source text. The degree to which a translator has succeeded in this task is clearly demonstrable with regard to impersonal, factual writing.

1.2   Language and Choice

Communication is basic to all human communities and, according to McEldowney (1990:13), can be broadly defined as *the process by which information is exchanged*. She indicates that there are many ways in which communication takes place – through spoken language, through written language, through signs, through sound, through gesture, through facial expression and so on. It is, however, communication through language which is the central concern here.

In the twentieth century, there was continuous exploration of the way language is used and several bodies of theory were developed and applied to linguistic research. Very early on, structural linguistics saw language as a system of structures or signs, a view first put forward in Sassure's *Course in General Linguistics* (1916). Amongst other things, Sassure made an important distinction between **langue** and **parole**. Langue is the code or the system which language users in a particular speech community use while parole refers to the individual utterances made in the system. Parole indicates those particular formal aspects of the system that individual users choose as appropriate for a particular situation. The linguist, however, was not concerned with describing parole but with describing langue.

In 1957, in *Syntactic Structures*, Chomsky described language as the knowledge of the system and saw the knowledge of this system as innate and universal. He made a distinction between **competence** and **performance**. Competence is defined as the unconscious knowledge of the ideal speaker while performance is the actual use of the language. Again, the linguist was not concerned with performance or actual language use but with trying to create rules to account for linguistic competence.

The 1960's saw the rise of functionalism which, according to Lyons (1981:224), was characterised by the belief that the particular language structures used are *determined by the functions that they have to perform*. Within this school, Halliday (1985) was interested in relating the structures of the language to semantic and social factors. There was a shift from examining the system of a language to an interest in how it is used. In this context, Searle (1969) on speech acts and Grice (1975) on conversational implicature, focus on the pragmatic analysis of language. They examine aspects of meaning which are derived from the way in which utterances are used and how they are related to the context in which they are uttered.

In thinking about language in the context of translation, it is clear that it is not the system that is of significance but, rather, the emphasis must be on how the language is used on particular occasions. It is clear that written language is used to serve various communicative purposes under a wide range of conditions. Because of this variety, there is an enormously wide range of options for the writer to choose from in producing text. A study of written text at large, however, allows us to draw out systematic regularities though, the more a writer is concerned with conveying concrete, world knowledge, the more obvious are these regularities. The characteristic selection of options chosen by a writer in the effort to achieve successful communication is often referred to as **style**. For instance, Milic (1971: 77-94) says that style results from the selection of options offered by the language. Darbyshire (1971:78) suggests that

> *Style in the use of language is a deviation from a norm and that there are good social reasons why such deviations should exist for language is to be found only in its uses in the actuality of the world, and not in the imagination of those who might see nothing more than its possibility.*

Leech & Short (1981) provide a general interpretation of style, stating that the term *refers to the way in which language is used in a given context, by a given person, for a given purpose, and so on.*

The notion of style, however, has been applied more specifically in a literary context. For instance, Gray (1984:277) indicates that style is the characteristic manner in which individual writers express themselves. He also indicates, however, that the notion is used to refer to the unique features of an individual literary work. In addition, Beaugrande & Dressler (1981:16) indicate that a style can be identified for *a group of texts by similar authors* and that we can also identify the style *of representative texts for an entire historical period and even of texts typical of an overall culture.*

The point is that certain features can be isolated to describe the choices made by a single writer and also the choices which are typical of a group of writers.

In identifying the characteristic manner in which individual writers express themselves, Gray (1984:277) looks for *a combination of many different factors, such as typical syntactical structures, a favourite or distinctive vocabulary, or kinds of imagery, attitude to subject matter, kind of subject matter, and so on.* At the other end of the scale, McEldowney is concerned with identifying general trends for the purpose of language learning and translation. Of linguistic communication, she says that the grammar of a language is the code for encoding and decoding messages in either spoken or written form. Thus, she believes that *different communicative purposes can be identified according to the cluster of linguistic features conventionally chosen by speakers of the language involved* (1990:49).

In her various writings, an examination of syntactic features in text enables McEldowney to identify, for instance, language which **instructs** people to do things, language which **narrates** a series of events and language which **describes** things, people, needs, thoughts, ideas, philosophies. She then goes on to consider text from the point of view of how the grammatical features chosen deviate from "the norm" she has established together with features like choice of lexis, the degree of personal involvement of the writer, the degree of abstraction of concepts expressed and the like. This enables her to identify *three central types of language* which she typifies as *social language, figurative language typical of imaginative creation* and *neutral, expository, transactional language* (1994:2).

1.3   Predictability

As indicated in the previous section, human communication is motivated by a need to accumulate and impart information. The more cohesive and coherent a text produced for this purpose, the more comprehensible it will be. Quirk (1968:237), however, suggests that *ease of comprehension must take place in the queue with other priorities...It should never be willfully or carelessly neglected. We should care for the ease and comfort of the receivers.* In this respect, as referred to above with regard to McEldowney's work, it is possible to establish norms as to the way in which information is communicated and, in general terms, the more closely a piece of writing adheres to those norms the more immediately comprehensible it is.

Such immediate comprehensibility is related to the impersonal nature of the language which is conventionally used to communicate what the writer regards to be factual information. A text written in this way, which cannot be attributed to a particular writer and which does not give rise to a debate about meaning (Text 1 in 1.4), is unlikely to attract the attention of a student of stylistics. The text is appreciated in terms of the reader's interest in the informational content and the explicitness with which it is expressed. As suggested in the previous section, however, there are thousands of deviations from the norm, ranging from *le criteaux* of the streets to the greatest works of literature and once the norms are flouted, a study of stylistics becomes the focus of attention.

The translation of literary texts involves an examination of what their writers have done with the language for the purpose of achieving an aesthetic effect. For this purpose it is important to see how the language, both syntactically and at the level of the word, deviates from what is normally expected. As a means towards this end, however, knowledge of such "normal" language must be developed. It can be seen as a control agent.

Where English is the source language, the English comprehension skills of some trainee translators may still need practice. An important by-product of learning to translate can be the enhancement of the trainees' reading skills with regard to English text. In this respect, factual, impersonal text is central for learners of English as a foreign language. McEldowney (1996/7:4) argues that, as factual language *is predictable in both form and vocabulary*, it is most immediately learnable and that *once it is learned* such factual language *can be the medium* for learning less predictable forms of the language.

1.4   Factual (Transactional) Language

The purpose of the following text is to impart information about Charlemagne in a straightforward way, the language being used merely as a carrier of facts.

> ### Text 1
> *Eleven centuries ago one man ruled most of Western Europe. Charlemagne could hardly read or write, yet he built up a vast empire. Charlemagne was a Frank, one of the people who had invaded the Roman Empire when it collapsed in the 5th century and who then settled in northern France. He was a great warrior. When he became king in AD 768, his territory was small and threatened by its French neighbours. Charlemagne soon overcame them and invaded northern Italy. (Children's Illustrated Encyclopaedia, 1991:107).*

Such text can be seen as *committed to the organisation of the real world* (Beaugrande & Dressler, 1981:160). Expectations of what readers can extract from this text are more or less defined – three events in Charlemagne's life, three events in the settlement of the Franks, descriptive information about Charlemagne and the situation in western Europe eleven centuries ago. This information is conveyed in linguistic forms[1] identified by McEldowney (1996/7) as being typical of these purposes.

The three dynamic, stem+*ed* (past tense) verb forms *became, overcame, invaded,* for instance, indicate a sequence of events related to Charlemagne becoming king and extending his empire. Three similar forms, *collapsed, invaded, settled* indicate another sequence related to the collapse of the Roman Empire and the invasion of the Franks which historically preceded Charlemagne's rise to fame.

We note that, with regard to this latter sequence, the events are not related in the order in which they actually happened. This is clearly marked, however, by the use of *had* and *when* to indicate that the collapse of the Roman Empire happened before the invasion. There are also the sequence markers *then* and *soon* to double-mark the order in which the events occurred. The verbs in these sequences occur in typical clausal patterns, maintaining the predominant subject/verb/complement order of English sentences. In this text we find SV(A) – *it / collapses / in the 5ᵗʰ century* and *who / settled / in northern France* and SVO – *Charlemagne / overcame / them* and *(he) / invaded / northern Italy*. The sentences are relatively balanced in length.

---

[1] Clusters of particular verb forms, verb types, sentence patterns and textual organisation of information are matched with particular communicative purposes. See Chapter 2 for a detailed description of these.

The features just illustrated are those which McEldowney indicates to be the norm for expressing the communicative purpose of "narrative". She also indicates that it is normal for such sequences of happenings to be padded out by descriptive language using, for instance, the stem+*ed* form of stative verbs like *was* in sentences of the form SVC – *Charlemagne / was / a Frank* and *his territory / was / small.*

Text 1 cannot be attributed to any particular writer because it does not use any special features that enable us to identify its writer. The pattern illustrated in one that, according to McEldowney (1990), re-occurs with great frequency throughout educational texts and general informational texts written in English. The type of language introduced here is dealt with in greater detail in Chapter Two.

1.5   Meaning & Transactional Language

If a reader comes across an unfamiliar word in a transactional text, it is likely that its meaning can be identified in a dictionary. It is important to understand, however, that the predictable nature of transactional language allows a reader, who is in control of the grammatical system of a language, to retrieve the meaning of an unfamiliar item from context. Let us first examine this with regard to English.

Let us imagine that in the following extract from Text 15 (2.2.4)

The bush baby mates at the end of the rains, so the breeding season depends on the local climate. The dominant male monitors the receptive state of the females in the group and when one becomes fertile he will not leave her until they have mated.

Four months after mating, the female gives birth in a nest some distance from the male ....

a translator is not familiar with the word *mate* in the context *The bush baby mates at the end of the rains, so the breeding season depends on the local climate.* The position of the word *mate* between the noun group *the bush baby* functioning as subject and *at the end of the rains* signalling "when" indicates that, here, the form *mates* is a verb. The following idea about the dependence of the breeding season on the climate is linked back to the action of mating in a result relationship by *so*. Thus, there is a result relationship between mating and breeding. Following items like *male, the receptive state of the female* and *fertile* all add information to make the concept of mating even clearer. Moreover, the repetition of *mate* in *he will not leave her till they have mated* sheds further light on the meaning. Finally, *four months after mating, the female gives birth* marks giving birth to be a result of mating. The former experience of most readers will allow them to hypothesise the meaning of *to mate* in this context.

Further elements of a chain through which the clarification of meaning develops can be seen in Text 15 with *the end of the rains* and *the local climate* linked by the result marker *so*. Another example is the occurrence of *adolescence, development, mature, continue to grow, develop* or the concepts of *fertile female, mating, giving birth, tiny offspring, nursing the young* all linked in a sequence of steps which the syntax marks (as outlined below in 2.2.4) that the description of a natural process is unfolding. As a text develops there is an ongoing process of the communication of meaning. There is a progression in which the linguistic devices involved signal relations within or among events and situations of the textual world (Beaugrande & Dressler, 1981:80). The essentially logical and semantic relations within transactional texts provide a coherent internal structure which allows for a high degree of predictability on the part of the translator. The same is true of transactional Arabic texts. For instance, in the following text about oil and natural gas in Algeria,

البترول والغاز الطبيعي من أهم مصادر الطاقة في الجزائر. وهما يشكلان الثروة الرئيسية للبلاد، غير أن مدخرات الغاز الطبيعي أكبر من مدخرات البترول، إذ تصل حوالي 2,8% من احتياطي العالم. ويتوفر الفحم أيضا ، لكن تكاليف استغلاله مرتفعة. أما الكهرباء فيتم توليد القسط الأكبر منها في المراكز الحرارية ، لضعف استثمار إمكانات البلاد من الكهرباء المائية.

الجغرافيا للسنة السابعة – المملكة المغربية 1997، ص74
(Geography for Year 6, The Kingdom of Morocco)

[Crude oil and natural gas are the main sources of energy in Algeria. They are also the main source of wealth in the country. The reserves of natural gas are much greater than those of crude oil and form 2.8% of world reserves. There is also coal, but the cost of production is very high. As for electricity, most of it is generated in the power plants because of the lack of we note that the dictionary meaning of طاقة includes 'energy', 'power', 'capacity', 'faculty', 'endurance', 'bearing' or 'an opening in a wall' (like a small window). If the reader is not familiar with the word, an appropriate meaning can be inferred from the context. For instance, items like petrol, natural gas, electricity, coal will indicate a narrowing down of the options to 'power' and 'energy'. Then, forms like مصادر ("sources") and الثروة("wealth") will lead the reader to narrow down the choice still further, more precisely to 'energy'.

Thus, each item provides the environment for what comes next. According to Halliday & Hasan (1985:48), this sets up internal expectations; and these are matched up with the expectations...that the listener or reader brings from external sources, from the context of situation and of culture. It is important to note, however, that the degree of dependence on culture with regard to external sources is relatively less with regard to transactional language than with literary language. The predictability of the form of transactional language signals the relationship between vocabulary items with clarity. This means that explanations are most often easily found from within rather than from outside a text. Further, the content of a transactional text is likely to be deeply rooted in world knowledge which means that external emotional and cultural experience is not such an important factor in the identification of meaning as it might be in a literary text.

1.6   Literary Language

As we have seen, the transactional mode, as illustrated by the Charlemagne text, is neutral with regard to person, culture and style. This lessens the complexity of decoding the information involved. The same cannot be said, however, of literary text which, by its very nature, depends on personal interpretation. For instance, Text 2 below, like the Charlemagne text above, involves narrative sequence with descriptive comment. Virginia Woolf has, however, chosen to communicate the events in a much more complex manner.

> ### Text 2
> (6) Macalister's boy took one of the fish and cut a square out of its side to bait his hook with. The mutilated body (it was alive still) was thrown back into the sea.
> (7) "Mrs. Ramsy!" Lily cried, "Mrs Ramsy!" but nothing happened. The pain increased, That anguish could reduce one to touch a pitch of imbecility, she thought! Anyhow the old man had not heard her. He remained benignant, calm – if one chose to think it – sublime. Heaven be praised, no one heard her cry that ignominious cry, stop pain. Stop! She had not obviously taken leave of her senses. She remained a skimpy old maid, holding a paint brush on the lawn. (Woolf, Triad Grafton Edition:195).

There is much greater linguistic variety illustrated in the extract from *To the Lighthouse*. For instance, initially, in (6) the sequence of happenings is related in much the same way as in the

Charlemagne text. The dynamic stem+*ed* verbs *took* and *cut* in straightforward SVO clauses outline two steps in the order they happened. This narration by the writer of what the boy did to the fish is then mingled with Lily's stream of consciousness in (7) as she reacts to the boy's actions. The writer does not intervene with expressions like *she thought* or *she felt* nor does she challenge Lily's own estimation of herself as a *skimpy old maid.*

This move from outlining the events which triggered Lily's feelings through the writer's eye to Lily's mental turmoil, the two linked by the description of the fish as *the mutilated body (it was alive still)*, is much more effective in depicting Lily's feelings. The reader is much more caught up in her feelings of horror and panic than would be the case if the writer had continued in the manner of the Charlemagne text – *Macalister's boy took one of the fish and cut a square out of its side to bait his hook. The fish was still alive when he threw it back into the sea. Lily was horrified by this.*

An awareness of the intensity of Lily's feelings of abandonment is developed in a similar way. The use of direct speech in *"Mrs Ramsy!" "Mrs Ramsy!"*, as Lily calls out for help, blends immediately into the indirect style *but nothing happened* – a move from outside reality to inner turmoil. This has a greater intensity than would a narration of the steps in the manner of the Charlemagne text – *Lily called out for Mrs Ramsy but no one responded.* The tumultuous emotions swarming in Lily's head sweep the reader along as short abrupt comments are inserted into a framework of much longer sentences - *...but nothing happened. The pain increased.* And *...stop pain, stop!*

This variety of form requires much more effort on the part of the reader in the search for meaning than was the case with the much more uniform type of expression illustrated by the Charlemagne text. It also contributes to a uniqueness with regard to Virginia Woolf's style. Though other writers may use similar effects, the exact effect made by the complexity of her narration here is not likely to be exactly reproduced by another writer.

The use of lexis in the Woolf extract also puts a greater demand on the reader than that of the Charlemagne text. The transactional text does not go beyond a surface referential meaning. There is nothing to imply beyond the facts that are stated. In the second text, however, Virginia Woolf makes much use of metaphor to heighten the artistic effect. For instance, for anguish to *reduce one to touch a pitch of imbecility* or to cause one to *step off ... into the waters of annihilation,* is much more evocative of strong emotional response than would be something like *she was surprised that the boy's action made her feel mentally unbalanced.*

This uniqueness of individual literary styles, in strong contrast with transactional language which recurs with very little variation, is an important marker of the genre and can, perhaps, be best illustrated by looking at another example.

Text 3

He crouched down between the sheets, glad of their tepid glow. He heard the fellows talk among themselves about him as he dressed for mass. It was a mean thing to do, to shoulder him into the square ditch, they were saying.

Then their voices ceased; they had gone. A voice at his bed said:

- *Dedalus, don't spy on us, sure you won't?*
Wells's face was there. He looked at it and saw that Wells was afraid.

- *I didn't mean to. Sure you won't*
His father had told him, whatever he did, never to peach on a fellow.
He shook his head and answered no and felt glad.

- *I didn't mean to, honour bright. It was only for a cod. I'm sorry.*
The face and the voice went away. Sorry because he was afraid. Afraid that it was some disease. Canker was a disease of plants and cancer one of animals: or another different. That was a long time ago then out on the playgrounds in the evening light, creeping from point to point on the fringe of his line, a heavy bird flying low through the grey light. Leicester Abbey lit up. Wolsey died there. The abbots buried him themselves. (Joyce, Wordsworth Edition:14)

Linguistically speaking, Text 3 illustrates a narrative with descriptive detail as do both Texts 1 and 2. We have already seen how Virginia Woolf's narrative deviated from the norm represented by the transactional information about Charlemagne. Joyce's narration deviates from both, however, indicating how unique is the style of each literary text. In this respect, Van Dijk (1972:IX.9) says that literary texts do not conform to the conventions of grammar and meaning in spite of the fact that they are written in the same language. This uniqueness is potentially the main source of enjoyment and artistic satisfaction for the reader in the same way as is the case with regard to a painting or piece of music.

Joyce, like Woolf, uses a complexity of devices to develop the narrative. The first two sentences are relatively straightforward narrative as in the Charlemagne text and the beginning of the Woolf text. Then, without any conventions to show that what is being related is direct speech, we get *It was a mean thing to do, to shoulder him into the square ditch.* The reader has to make a mental leap to make the connection intended. What follows is a medley of direct speech and indirect style contrasting Wells' words with the thoughts they spark off in the other man's mind. Then follows a section, after Wells has left the room, which illustrates an important feature of Joyce's writing. Such a set of apparently disconnected sentences is unique to Joyce.

Speaking of transactional text, Beaugrande & Dressler (1981:5) say that *cause, enablement and reason have forward directionality, that is, the earlier event or situation causes, enables or provides the reason for the later one.* This is quite clear with regard to the straightforward, chronological development of the Charlemagne text. The Woolf text in this respect, however, relies on a repetition of the same idea, that of Lily losing her mind at the horror of the boy's action with regard to the fish. There is not a straightforward chronological development at this point. When speaking of Woolf's style in this respect. Marsh (1998:169) speaks of the chaotic detail of incidents that chime and fill the air with vibrations. Joyce, however, relies on word association. *I'm sorry...Sorry because he was afraid. Afraid that it was some disease. Canker was a disease of plants and cancer one of animals*, for instance, and the reader has to work hard to interpret what is going on.

Thus it can be seen that it is the purpose of the writer that determines the different characteristics that enable us to distinguish transactional language from literary language and that enable us to identify individual literary styles. At one extreme we have a concern with the communication of facts in a conventional, familiar manner. Meaning is communicated in a systematic and predictable way. At the other extreme we find unique pieces of art. Each literary style presents a unique syntactic pattern and, speaking of how the writer organises the world that is the literary text, Freeman (1975:20) says that each *reflects cognitive preferences, a way of seeing the world; perhaps more importantly, it reflects the fundamental principles of artistic design.* A literary style can thus be established for particular writers so that we can refer to Virginia Woolf's style, James Joyce's style, Jane Austin's style, Charles Dickens' style and so on. The way an individual writer's work coheres is marked by a combination of features of the type briefly illustrated above and which will be detailed further below when we investigate the complexity of literary texts.

1.7 ⋙ *Try This (1)*

Language Variation

Look at Texts (a) – (c) and complete the table below by ticking (✓) the appropriate boxes

> ***Text (a)***
> A.   How do you do? You from around here?
> B.   No, this is my first time.
> A.   How are you finding it – a bit damp and chilly?
> B.   Not bad really. Could be worse.
> A.   Yes. We were lucky this month actually. Probably be a change for the worse soon.
>
> ***Text (b)***
> Very early morning. The sun not yet risen and the whole bay hidden   under a swirling mist. Everything unreal, ethereal. Ghostly shapes looming and receding. The tone of the day was set.
>
> ***Text (c)***
> The weather in the capital is changeable This is especially so in the winter months. In December, for instance, there were day-to-day temperature changes of several degrees. Similarly, sun, wind, cloud, fog, rain and snow were all recorded. Thus, film scheduling is very difficult.

Table: Language Variation

		Text (a)	Text (b)	Text (c)
Mode	Written			
	Spoken			
Subject Matter	Central			
	Peripheral			
Where	Report			
	Textbook			
	Novel			
	Social Gathering			
Purpose	Educating			
	Setting a Scene			
	Imparting Facts			
	Drawing Characters			
	Stimulating the Imagination			
	Socialising			
Style	Personal			
	Impersonal			
	Subjective			
	Objective			
Syntax	Unpredictable			
	Predictable			
	Systematic			
	Fragmentary			
	Complete			
Lexis	Concrete			
	Abstract			
	Idiomatic			
Best Description	Social			
	Factual			
	Literary			
Possible Translation	Homogeneous			
	Various			
	Individualistic			

➜ Now turn to the **KEY.**

1.8   Conclusion

When we consider the stylistic differences we have been discussing, it is clear that the reader has a different role with regard to impersonal language communicating fact and that which is more personal. This has obvious implications for the translator. Each translator will approach a literary text in an individual way. Each translator will respond to the text differently and we can expect each translation to be unique. On the other hand, different attempts to translate the same transactional text are likely to show a greater degree of homogeneity[2].

---

[2] Chapter 3 reports the findings of a small case study conducted to illustrate this point.

Chapter Two
Transactional Text:
Communicative Purposes

2.1   Introduction

Before considering the role of the translator with regard to factual or transactional text we need first to provide a textual description of the type that will allow us to see the nature of the "norm" with which we are dealing. Towards this end McEldowney's communicative purpose model (1990, 1994, 1996/7) provides an appropriate framework for revealing the coherence and cohesion typical of such discourse. It allows us to catalogue, for both English and Arabic, the linguistic markers which mark each of the communicative purposes she identifies and shows how meaning is communicated in transactional discourse.

2.2   Communicative Purposes

Transmitters of factual information might have the purpose of **instructing,** or of **narrating,** or of **describing,** three broad purposes which McEldowney (1990) identifies as being basic to most language communities. Each purpose can be identified by a typical cluster of linguistic features in both English and Arabic.

2.2.1 Instruction

Language can be used to tell people what to do, how to do it, what not to do and the like. Such instructions are essential in the day-to-day conduct of the life of a community. Further, according to McEldowney (1996/7:4), they are also a *central means of setting up learning tasks* in schools and also occur within subject content across the curriculum as, for instance, in setting up apparatus and conducting scientific experiments, information technology, cooking recipes, physical activities and games and so on.

Text 4 below illustrates a typical set of English instructions:

> **Text 4**
> *1   Mix all the ingredients together in the bowl. Use the knife to cut up the butter, then knead with your fingers until the flour and sugar are blended into the butter and the mixture is sticky.*
> *2   Tip the mixture out in front of you. Flatten it to about 1cm (½ in) thick. You may need to put flour on the work surface to keep the mixture from sticking. Use the cutter to make biscuits, and lay them on the baking tray. Make sure that the edges do not touch.*
> *3   Bake the biscuits at Gas Mark 4/250F/120C for about 20 minutes or until light brown. When you take them out of the oven, use a cloth or oven glove and place the tray on a wooden board so that the tray does not burn the work surface.* (Vorderman, 1997:57)

Here, the verbs *mix, use, tip, flatten*, etc are imperative. That is, according to McEldowney (1990), they are in the stem form in that they have no inflection and they are dynamic in that they refer to an action that is to be carried out.

Further, *sentences occur in pieces of discourse in particular patterns dependent on communicative purpose* (McEldowney (1996/7:4) and, in Text 4, they have no subject or doer of the action indicated by the verb. Besides the verbal component, instruction sentences may contain a "what" element or object like *all the ingredients* in *Mix all the ingredients in the bowl*. In addition, various adverbial elements occur expressing, for instance, "where" as *in front of you* in *Tip the mixture out in front of you*, "purpose" as *to cut up the butter* in *Use the knife to cut up the butter*, "how" as *with your fingers* in *Knead with your fingers* and so on. This results in sentences of two central types V (*Jump; Stand up)* and VO (*Make / some biscuits; Use / bleach)* most often, as in Text 4, with additional adverbial information as indicated above. A further feature of instruction sentences is that the reader may be addressed directly as with *you* in *You may need to put flour on the work surface.*

Also important is how sentences are organised within a piece of discourse. As indicated by McEldowney (1994), one type of instructions is marked by a sequence of sentences occurring in the sequence in which the steps involved are to be carried out. In Text 4, for instance, this sequence is indicated by the numbers 1 to 3 marking an overall sequence of mixing, shaping and then cooking, three processes that need to be carried out in that order if the biscuits are to be made successfully. Then, within each of these, there is a sequence of steps – for instance, in 2, *Tip out the mixture. Flatten it. Cut out the biscuits Lay them on the baking tray.*

We note, further, that, inserted into a sequence of occurrence involved in making the biscuits, may be "warnings" or comments on how to proceed. For instance, in Text 4 such a comment is illustrated by *Make sure that their edges do not touch* with reference to the step of laying the biscuits on the baking tray. Related to this, in fact, is another type of instruction identified by McEldowney (1990), as having the same verbal and sentence features as those described with regard to Text 4, but which is not sequenced according to the order in which steps are to be carried out. Rather, such instructions provide advice or a set of tips. For instance,

Text 5
Do not transfer into any other bottle.
Do not use on enamel or plated metal (chrome/gold) surface.
Do not use undiluted on floors.
Do not use on wool silk, coloureds, man-made fibres, leather or garments with a special finish e.g. flame proof. Always refer to the garment label.
Take care not to spill on fabric/furnishing/carpets or damage will result.
Always wipe up spillages and rinse thoroughly with clean water. Wash hands after use
(from a bottle of household bleach).

In such instructions the rationale for organisation is more a conceptual one, in this case "container", "surfaces", "garments", "furnishings", "cleaning up".

We also find instructions in Arabic with a typical set of linguistic markers. These can be exemplified by Text 6 which illustrates a set of sequenced instructions for cooking makluba and Text 7 which provides advice on how to look after ones eyesight.

Text 6

قشر الباذنجان وقطعه قطعا ، ثم رشه بالملح واتركه مدة ساعة أو انقعه بالماء والملح مدة ساعة ، ثم نشفه بمنشفة وبعد ذلك اقله بالسمن أو المار جرين ثم ضعه بالفرن وعليه شيئا من السمن واخبزه في فرن حام.

انقع الأرز بالماء المغلي ثم قشر رأسا من البصل وافرمه ريشا وقشر رأسا من الثوم . ثم أقل البصل بالسمن حتى يذبل ثم أضف اللحم والثوم وقلبه حتى يحمر ثم أضف ماء نصف الطنجرة واترك اللحمة تغلي مدة ...

(فن الطبخ والحلويات العربية ، سميرة ترمس . دار الهدى الوطنية 1985، ص 126)
(The Art of Arabic Cooking and Sweets, *Samira Termis, Dar Al-Huda Alwataniya, 1985:126*)

[Peel the aubergine and cut it into pieces. Then sprinkle it with salt and leave it for an hour or soak it in brine for an hour. Then dry it with a towel. After that fry it in butter or margarine and put it in the oven with some butter on the top. Bake it in a high oven.

Soak the rice in boiling water. Then peel an onion and chop it thinly. Peel a whole garlic bulb. Fry the onion in butter until it is soft and then add the meat and garlic. Stir until brown, add water half the pot and leave the meat to boil.] (Translated by Saad, 2002)

Text 7

في أثناء القراءة والكتابة استعمل ضوءا مناسبا ، لأن العمل في الضوء الضعيف يتعب العينين. عندما تشعر أنك لا ترى الأشياء بوضوح راجع الطبيب لفحص عينيك .
حافظ على نظافة النظارة الطبية ولا تعرضها للخدش .
راجع الطبيب باستمرار واتبع نصائحه.
(كتاب العلوم للصف الرابع الابتدائي ، المملكة الأردنية الهاشمية. مطبعة دار الكتب العلمية ـ 1995 صفحة 84)

(*The Science Book for Year 4,* Jordan, Dar Al-Kitab Al Wataniya, 1995: 84)

> *[Use suitable lighting when reading and writing because working in poor light weakens the eyes.*
> *See a doctor for a sight test when you feel you do not see clearly.*
> *Keep your spectacles clean and do not let them get scratched.*
> *Visit your doctor regularly and follow his advice.]*
> (Translated by Saad, 2002)

In the recipe illustrated in Text 6, the verbs: قشر-قطع-رش-اترك-نشف- اقل-ضع اخبز-انقع..الخ are in the imperative mode in which the reader may be addressed directly. As in the case of the English recipe illustrated above in Text 4, the Arabic imperative forms are dynamic, indicating a series of steps to be carried out by the reader. Unlike English, the verbs are marked for person. In the version above the masculine singular is used to address a general reader, whether male or female[3]. The sentences are of one central

---

[3] It is to be noted, however, that when asked to translate Text 4 into Arabic, a female translator used the feminine, perhaps because her assumption was that, in the Arab culture, a female is more likely to make biscuits than is a man.

VO type – قشر الباذنجان with additional adverbial information. Thus we find the expression of "where" inبالفرن وضعه   "purpose" in حتى يذبل and "how" as in افرمه ريشا. The sentences in the text are organised according to the sequence in which the steps in the recipe should be carried out. This involves dealing with the aubergine, preparing the rice and onion, preparing the meat, putting all the ingredients into a copper pot and finally, turning the mixture onto a tray.

Interspersed in the sequence of steps are "warnings" and comments on how to proceed to ensure a successful result. For instance, when all the ingredients are placed in the pot, the reader is advised not to stir them and the writer indicates the use of a copper pot without explanation. Such comments use the same type of verbs and sentences as those outlining the sequence. This is also the case regarding the instructions giving advice on looking after one's eyesight illustrated in Text 7. This advice is, as in the English example, organised according to concept. It moves from a discussion about light, to the need for seeing an optician, to how to care for spectacles and, finally, to advise about visiting a doctor regularly. A negative imperative لا تعرضها للخدش is expressed by the jussive preceded by لا 'do not'.

2.2.2 Narration

Besides being a vehicle for telling people what to do, language is also used to relate what has happened to people and communities.

In this respect the communicative purpose identified by McEldowney (1990) as narrative outlines a series of incidents and events in such a way as to emphasise the chronological sequence of the happenings. A factual narrative may outline people's lives and experiences, outline developments within communities with regard to industry, art, craft and the like, trace the development of world conflicts and so on. As in the case of instruction, in its transactional realisation, a set of predictable linguistic markers can be identified for narration. For instance, in Text 8 below, the sequence of dynamic verbs *arrived, begged, decided, went, tended* in the stem +*ed* form (or the past tense) outline a series of steps that are said to have been carried out.

> **Text 8**
> *At about seven o'clock, just after dawn, a strange deputation arrived at the mission compound. They were Chinese armed to the teeth, on a mission of mercy. They knew the Bishop had some medicines and they begged him to go with them to the hospital, where some thirteen or fourteen Chinese lay wounded. The Bishop decided to trust them, went to the hospital and tended to the wounded.*
> (Payne, 1960:91)

The verbs are preceded in their sentences by the doers of the actions involved. The patterns illustrated in the text are SV (*a strange deputation / arrived*), SVO (*The Bishop / decided / to trust them*) and SVOO (*They / begged / him / to go with them to the hospital ....*). Fitted around these basic sentence patterns may be adverbial groups expressing concepts of "time" (*at about* seven o'clock), "place" (*at the mission compound*) and the like. Within texts like this, the sentences involved are related in the order in which the events actually happened.

The Arabic illustrated in Text 9 below similarly outlines a series of events in a chronological sequence.

Text 9

ومات الإمبراطور لويس سنة 840 ، فوقع الخلاف بين أولاده ، واغتنم عبد الرحمن هذه الفرصة، فأرسل المسلمين لغزو فرنسا ،فدخلوا من مصب نهر الرون ، وعاثوا في مدينة آرل ونواحيها. وبعث العساكر بقيادة موسى بن موسى ، عامل تطيلة ، فراحوا يتقدمون حتى بلغوا ارض برطانية. والتقى المسلمون بالفرنسيين فلم يستطع الفرنسيون صبرا فانهزموا وعاد موسى بالغنائم والأسلاب .

(العرب في أوروبا _ عبد الرحمن و طرف ـ تأليف: عبد الحميد جودة السحار،مكتبة مصر ،صفحة 7 .لا يوجد تاريخ نشر)

(*Arabs In Europe, Abdul-Rahman and Taraf,* by Abdul-Hameed Juda Assahar.Maktabat Mesr, page 7. (There is no publication date.)

[Emperor Louis died in 840. Disputes broke out between his sons. Abdul Rahman seized the opportunity and sent Moslems to invade France. They attacked from the river mouth of Rhõne . They ransacked the city of Earle and its outskirts. He sent soldiers led by Mousa Bin Mousa the governor of Tatila. They advanced till they reached the land of Britannia. The Moslems engaged with the French. The French could not resist and they retreated. Mousa returned with spoils and loot.] (Translated by Saad, 2002)

Here, the narrative, which outlines the death of Emperor Louis of France in the year 840, the following disagreement among his sons, the invasion by a Muslim army, the defeat of the French and the resulting plunder and pillage. The sequence of dynamic verbs in the past tense outline the series of steps

مات، وقع، اغتنم،أرسل، دخل، عاث، بعث..الخ

Unlike the order of elements in English narrative sentences, here, the sentences are of the VS form مات الإمبراطور , the VSO form وقع ـ فأرسل المسلمين لغزو فرنسا - and the VSOO form الخلاف بين وأولاده

That is, in Arabic, verbal sentences are used to narrate a series of events.

We note in Text 8 above that, as well as the narrative sequence we have identified, there are also descriptive comments. For instance, *They were Chinese armed to the teeth* and *They knew the Bishop had some medicines* describe the Chinese deputation. Here, the stem +*ed* forms *were* and *knew* do not refer to a step in a sequence of events but, in this context, are stative. Similarly, in Text 9 we note a descriptive in the Arabic sentence وبعث العساكر بقيادة موسى بن موسى to clarify the leader's identity.

It is common to find such stative comments interspersed throughout narrative sequences for the purpose of describing the appearance and feelings of characters, setting the scene and so on. For instance, Text 10 below is a descriptive section in what is basically a narrative account of the life of Emily Hobhouse.

2.2.3   Stative Description

Text 10

After the death of her mother, Emily with her sister Maude were responsible for the welfare of their father. She felt trapped but remained a dutiful daughter. Emily was a good organiser and helped in parish work. This involved a lot of walking which gave her a sense of freedom and she was also able to meet local people. It gave her a lifelong sympathy for the poor people. (Holt, 2000:30)

Here, we note that the central purpose is to describe a period in Emily's life. The past tense verbs *were, was, helped, involved, gave, was, gave* are stative in that, in this context, they function in sentences describing the responsibility of Emily, Maude and parish work. The sentences involved begin with the person or thing being described and occur in patterns SVC (*Emily and her sister Maude / were / responsible for the welfare of their father*), SVO (*This / involved / a lot of walking*), SVOO (*It / gave / her / a lifelong sympathy for the poor people*). Adverbial elements expressing, for instance, concepts like "time" (*after the death of her mother*) may be added to the sentences.

As the verbs are stative, the sentences are not arranged in the discourse according to a sequence of occurrence. Rather, *the organisation can be said to be according to concept* (McEldowney, 1990:17). Here, for instance, the opening section of three sentences is devoted to Emily as a daughter. The following section is concerned with Emily's role in the parish concluding with a remark looking forward to the rest of her life.

Similarly, in Arabic we find sections of description related to narrative sequences. For instance, in Text 11

Text 11

كنت أدخن مائة وعشرين سيجارة في اليوم، ولم اكن استعمل عوداًالكبريت إلا مرة أو مرتين في اليوم . وذات لبلة في شهر ديسمبر كانت الأمطار تسقط بغزارة في القاهرة وأصوات الرعد والبرد تهز فراشي، واستيقظت لأدخن سيجارة وفوجئت أن البيت ليس فيه سيجارة واحدة. وكانت الساعة الرابعة صباحا فقمت من فراشي وارتديت ملابسي ووضعت حول عنقي كوفية من الصوف وغطيت نفسي بمعطف ثقيل ونزلت إلى الشارع ابحث عن دكان سجائر اشتري منه الدخان أو فاعل خير يمشي في الشارع اشحذ منه سيجارة. ووجدت كل الدكاكين مغلقة ولم أجد أحدا في الشارع يدخن سيجارة وركبت سيارتي ومضيت ابحث عن محل سجائر مفتوح ، وبعد نصف ساعة وجدت محلا في ميدان التحرير واشتريت منه علبة سجائر. وعدت إلى بيتي وفي فمي سيجارة وكنت أسعد رجل في العالم ولكن عدت ومعي برد شديد أبقاني في الفراش سبعة أيام.

(Hatim, 1994: 127)

[I was smoking 120 cigarettes in a day, and I hardly ever used a match, apart from once or twice a day. One night in December it was raining heavily in Cairo. The thunderstorm was shaking my bed and so I woke up to smoke a cigarette but to my surprise there was not a single cigarette in the house. It was 4:00 am in the morning so I got out of bed, put on my clothes, wrapped a woollen scarf around my neck, put on a heavy coat and set off out of my house in search of cigarettes, either from a shop or a good-doer.

I found that all the shops were closed and no one was smoking on the street. So I got into my car and again I went in search of cigarettes. After half an hour I found a shop in Tahrir Square and I bought a packet of cigarettes. I headed back to my house with a cigarette in my mouth and I was the happiest man in the world but when I came back with a cold that kept me in bed for seven days.]

(Translated by Saad, 2002)

We find descriptive information about the writer's smoking habit in general and comments about a particular occasion on which he went out in a thunderstorm to get some cigarettes. Here the verbs كنت أدخن، لم أكن استعمل، كانت الأمطار، استيقظت لأدخن ، فوجئت، وجدت كل الدكاكين، لم أجد أحد في الشارع. are in the past tense but they are stative, rather than narrative.

Verbs such as نزلت، غطيت ، وضعت ، ارتديت ملابسي، قمت من فراشي ، ركبت سيارتي ، مضيت ، وجدت محلا، عدت إلى بيتي، كنت أسعد رجل، عدت أبقاني في الفراش ومعي برد، however, are narrative occurring in a chronological sequence.

The sentences are verbal, occurring in the patterns VO (استيقظت)
VSO
VSOC (ركبت سيارتي) (كنت أدخن مائة سيجارة في اليوم)

As well as the type of stative description discussed above as being related to narrative sequences we also find free-standing description in both English and Arabic. For instance, Text 12 is centrally a description of the guinea pig and its care in captivity and, as such, illustrates the linguistic features of this communicative purpose.

Text 12
The correct name for a guinea pig is a cavy. The more hardy smooth-haired kinds are best for beginners to keep. Cavies like raised cages similar to rabbit hutches, with hay

for sleeping. They eat little and often: fresh greens, carrots, turnips, apple peel, bread and special mix from the pet shop. In summer they can crop the grass in the garden – but enclose and protect them. They like a hot bran mash meal at night in winter, but do not let them get fat. They need plenty of water, changed each day, from a larger water bottle. If cared for, a cavy can live for up to eight years.
(Hamlyn, 1985:117)

Here, as in Text 10, the verbs do not refer to actions. They are stative. They are, however, different in form to those discussed above with regard to the description associated with narrative. In free-standing description of the type illustrated by the guinea pig example, the verbs are in "the simple present". In McEldowney's terminology, *is* represents the stem+*s* form, the *–s* inflection showing concord with "third person singular" (*he/she/it)* subjects. Verbs like *are, like, eat, can, need* are in the stem form.

The sentences in free-standing stative description are similar to those we saw with regard to Text 10 and those illustrated here are SVA (*Cavies / eat / often)*, SVO (*Cavies / like / raised cages)* and SVC (*The correct name for a guinea pig / is / a cavy.*) Adverbial elements occur around these basic patterns to express "where" (*They can crop grass **in the garden***), "when" (*They like a hot bran mash meal **at night in winter.***).

In the text, the overall purpose of which is to describe how to keep guinea pigs as pets, sentences are organised, as indicated with regard to Text 10, according to a conceptual rationale. As an introduction, the first sentence expresses "name" and the second goes on to identify "type" for beginners to keep. The rest of the text is devoted to aspects of care – "living conditions", "eating needs",` "drinking needs", "life expectancy". Within the section related to eating needs, the concepts are "amount", "frequency", "food", "summer eating", "winter eating" and, finally, a return to "amount". The coherence of the text would be damaged if, for instance, the information about eating were scattered throughout the text rather than all gathered together in one section or if the naming of the animal and the appropriate type to keep were to follow information about care.

The description we have here is making a generalisation about guinea pigs and, as such, can be said to be general in reference. In contrast, the description about Emily and Maude in Text 10 above is about two particular people at a particular stage in their lives and can, therefore, be said to be specific in reference. We note further, that, in both English and Arabic, free-standing, specific description can also be specific. For instance, Text 13 is a specific description in English of the Planet Jupiter while Text 14 is a specific description in Arabic of Halley's Comet.

Text 13
Jupiter is the largest planet of all. It has a diameter 11 times that of the Earth. Like the other giant planet, it is mostly a ball of hydrogen and helium. This is in the form of gas at the surface, but deeper down the gas is packed together so thickly that it becomes more like a liquid than a

gas. At the centre is a core of hot, molten rock.
(Stannard, 1996:26)

Text 14

مذنب هالي ومداره:

هذا المذنب المدهش يدور حول الشمس مرة كل 76 سنة وسيظهر ثانية عام 1986. عندما يقترب مذنب هالي من الشمس يصبح ذنبه مرئيا. طرف الذيل دائما بعيدا عن الشمس.

[Halley's Comet and its Orbit
This astonishing comet orbits the sun once every 76 years. It will appear in the year 1986. When Halley's comet approaches the sun, its tail becomes noticeable and the tail is always to the other side of the sun.] (Translated by Saad, 2002)

As can be seen, verb form, verb type, sentence pattern and organisation of information are similar in both specific and general stative description.

2.2.4   Sequenced Description

As well as stative description, occurring in the ways indicated above, two types of sequenced description can be identified. These are description of natural processes and description of processes which occur through the intervention of man. Both are normally general in reference. The following text about bush babies, for instance, contains elements of sequenced description related to the process of reproduction.

Text 15
The bush baby mates at the end of the rains, so the breeding season depends on the local climate. The dominant male monitors the receptive state of the females in the group and

when one becomes fertile he will not leave her until they have mated.

Four months after mating, the female gives birth in a nest some distance from the male who might otherwise kill the unfamiliar-smelling young. The tiny offspring are fully-furred and born with their eyes open. The female nurses them for three days before venturing out to feed again. While foraging she either leaves the young in the nest or takes them with her, their tiny hands clinging to her coat.

The female returns with her offspring to the communal nest after 10 to 15 days, and her young are weaned at 11 weeks. The offspring have a surprisingly long adolescence, mainly due to the slow development of their brains. Although sexually mature at ten months, they continue to grow and develop, and males will probably not breed for several years (Wildlife Explorer, MCMXCVI, Pack 04)

Here, we find steps expressed sequentially in, for instance, The dominant male monitors the receptive state of the females in the group.... one becomes fertile...the female gives birth.... the female nurses them for three days ..the female returns with her offspring to the communal nest after 10 to 15 days...the offspring....continue to grow and develop. *That is, the stem and stem+s forms of dynamic verbs* (monitors, becomes, gives, nurses, returns, continue to grow, continue to develop) *relate a series of steps that recur in nature in sentence patterns similar to those described above with regard to narrative.*

Let us now look at the way natural process is expressed in Arabic.

Text 16

أن النبات يمتص الماء والأملاح المعدنية من التربة ، وغاز ثاني
أكسيد الكربون من   الهواء ليصنع منها المواد النباتية المختلفة ، بما فيها
المواد الغذائية ، وذلك بتأثير ضوء الشمس . وهكذا تنمو النباتات ، فتستهلك
قسما من المواد الغذائية ، وتختزن القسم الآخر منها في أعضائها المختلفة.
ويأتي دور الحيوانات آكلات الأعشاب ، فتأكل النباتات المختلفة ، وتحصل
منها على المواد الغذائية النباتية التي تساعدها على النمو والعيش. وهكذا
تتحول المواد الغذائية النباتية ، عن طريق آكلات الأعشاب ، إلى مواد
غذائية حيوانية.
والحيوانات آكلات اللحوم تفترس آكلات الأعشاب ،وتتغذى بالمواد الغذائية الحيوانية.

ونحن بدورنا نحصل على المواد الغذائية من النبات والحيوان، لأننا نأكل
الأطعمة النباتية ، والحيوانية .
فالإنسان إذن مزدوج التغذية ... كل ذلك مراحل هامة من دورة الغذاء في الطبيعة.
(العلوم للصف الرابع الابتدائي. وزارة المعارف في المملكة العربية السعودية. 1986.
صفحة51)

(*Our Arabic Language*, for Year 5. Ministry of Education in The
Kingdom of Jordan1996, page 48)

[A plant absorbs water and minerals from the soil, and takes in carbon
dioxide from the surrounding atmosphere to produce food by
photosynthesis. The plants grow, consuming part of the food and storing
the rest in different parts.
Now comes the role of herbivores. They eat different plants and absorb
the nutrients which help them to grow and survive. So nutrients from
plants are changed into animal nutrients by herbivores.
Carnivores eat herbivores because they eat meat. In turn, humans,
acquire nutrients from both plants and animals.
All these are important stages in the food chain in nature.]
    (Translated by Saad, 2002)

or

Text 17

إن نقطة الماء التي تجري في النهر أو الساقية ، تصل إلى البحر فتنضم إلى
مياهه.ثم تحولها أشعة الشمس بخارا يتصاعد في الجو ، فيلتقي هذا البخار

غيوما سارحة هناك. ثم إن برودة الجو الأعلى تحيلها إلى نقط ماء تتساقط على الأرض مطرا ، ينعش النبات والحيوان والبشر.
(لغتنا العربية-الصف الخامس، وزارة التربية في المملكة الأردنية الهاشمية - 1996.ص 48)

(*Our Arabic Language*, Year 5. Ministry of Education, The Kingdom of Jordan, 1996, page 48)

[Water which runs into a river or a stream reaches the sea.. The heat

of the sun evaporates it into steam which rises up. The steam meets

other drifting clouds. After that, the cold in the higher atmosphere

changes it into a drop of water again, falling as rain which gives life

to plants, animals and people.] (Translated by Saad, 2002)

The description of the food chain expressed in Arabic in Text 16 is a natural process, general in reference. The steps are expressed sequentially. First, for instance, plants take minerals from the soil and carbon dioxide from the air assisted by the sun in order to grow. Then animals feed on the plants and, in turn, meat-eating animals feed on the plant eaters. The verbs here يمتص، يصنع، ينمو، يستهلك، يخزن...الخ *are dynamic and in the present tense as they outline the steps in the cycle. In both parts of the text we note the recurrence of adverbial or quasi adverbial particles like* وهكذا، و...، ويأتي دور *which double mark the sequence like the English* then, next, after that *commonly occurring in chronologically sequenced language.*

The verbs expressing the steps in the cycle occur sometimes in nominal sentences – that is, SVO النبات يمتص الماء

and sometimes in verbal sentences VS يأتي دور الحيوانات and VSO فتأكل (هي) here هي is a hidden pronoun and subject which refers to النباتات المختلفة. Both Texts 16 and 17 begin with إن النبات in and إن. This item, translating as truly or certainly, introduces nominal sentences with the subject following in the accusative.

Finally, to complete our description of the communicative purposes to be found in transactional language, let us now turn to the description of man-controlled processes.

Text 18
To examine blood under the microscope a thin film must be spread on a slide. The finger is pricked with a sterile lancet which must be used by one person only. The drop of blood is placed at one end of a clean, dry slide. A second slide is placed as shown in Fig, 19.5 so that the blood drop spreads across the region of contact by capillary action. By pushing the top slide across the lower one, a thin film of blood is made which will show red cells quite clearly under the microscope. (Mackean, 1973:10)

Here, a sequence of steps carried out by the laboratory assistant in the process of making a blood smear is expressed by the sequence of passive verb groups – *is pricked, is placed, is placed, [is pushed] is made*. The sentences involved have centrally a "what" element functioning at S and "step" element functioning at V – *the finger / is pricked*. These elements may be completed by an adverbial element to express "agent" – *the finger is pricked* **with**

a sterile lancet, "where" *The drop of blood is placed **at one end***
of a clean, dry slide, "why" *A second slide is placed **so that the***
blood drop spreads across the region of contact ... and so on.

In Arabic, man-controlled process is expressed in the way illustrated below by Text 19.

Text 19

يمر إنتاج الإسمنت وتصنيعه بمراحل متعددة ؛ تبدأ بتحديد المنطقة التي تتوافر
فيها المواد الخام، لتحفر فيها آبار بأعماق مختلفة ، ثم تفجر للحصول على هذه
المواد وتنقل بقلابات عملاقة إلى الكسارات لتتحول إلى قطع صغيرة بحجم
البيضة أو أصغر قليلا ، ثم تجمع هذه المواد في حقل واسع وتخلط جيدا. ثم تطحن
وتعدل مكوناتها الرئيسية لضمان إنتاج نوعية ممتازة من المواد الناعمة. وتوضع
في خزان كبير ملحق بكل فرن ، وتخلط جيدا تمهيدا لحرقها بسهولة على درجة
عالية جدا ، لنحصل على الإسمنت...
(لغتنا العربية للصف الخامس- وزارة التربية ، المملكة الأردنية الهاشمية..1996
(Our Arabic Language, for Year 5. Ministry of (32 صفحة
Education, The Kingdom of Jordan1996, page 32)

[The production of cement passes through several stages. It starts
with identifying the sites rich in raw material. Mines are dug to
various depths. The rocks are dynamited and materials are taken away
in huge trucks to the crushers to change them into smaller pieces the
size of an egg or less. These materials are collected and spread out to
be well mixed. Then the material is ground. The main components are
modified to produce fine material. After that it is put in a big store
normally connected to a furnace. The materials are mixed well prior
to roasting them at very intense heat in order to obtain cement.]
(Translated by Saad, 2002)

Here, a sequence of steps carried out in making cement is outlined. After a stative sentence of introduction, يمر إنتاج الإسمنت

وتصنيعه، as in English, a sequence of passive verb groups تحول ،

تحفر ،تفجر، تنقل describes the steps in the process. The passive in

Arabic is termed مجهول (unknown). It is formed by changing the active form and adding the short vowel 'damma' on the first syllable. The form of the sentence is VO. As in English, various adverbials complete the process sentences to express, for instance, "agency"بقلابات تنقل , "where" في حقل "why"للحصول , "how".جيدا

2.3   📞 *Try This (2)*

Communicative Purposes (English)

1.   Look at texts (d) – (i) below and:

    (i)   identify the verbs and state their form.

    (ii)   identify the verb type as "dynamic" or "stative"

    (iii)   indicate whether the discourse is organised sequentially or conceptually

    (iv)   mark the sentence divisions and identify the sentence

            types as V, VA, VO, VO; SV, SVA, SVO, SVOA;

            SVC, *There*VC. (See Text (d))

    (v)   state the communicative purpose of each text as –

"instruction", "narrative", "stative description",

"description on natural process", "description of man-

controlled purpose".

Text (d)
Vernon arrived home from work and made a cup of coffee. He poured out a mugful and sat down to enjoy it. He took a sip. He smiled and began to relax and the various trials of the day receded.

Text (e)
The soil is prepared and holes are made at fixed intervals. Fertiliser is put into the holes and coffee seedlings are planted four to a hole. During the growing period they are carefully tended. When the coffee berries are mature they are picked by hand.

Text (f)
Measure the coffee into a warmed jug. Add the correct amount of boiling water and stir it well. Leave it for a minute and draw the edge of a spoon across the top. Stand the pot in a warm place for four minutes. Strain it and serve it.

Text (g)
The coffee plant produces white flowers. Soon the stigma receives pollen from the anthers and fertilisation occurs. Seeds develop and ripen. Some seeds find soil in which to grow and under suitable conditions a root bursts through the seed case and then a shoot develops.

Text (h)
There are many different types of coffee. They have different flavours. The coffees of Africa have a strong flavour. They are

often very bitter. Blue mountain coffee comes from Jamaica. It is a mixture of coffees and has an unusual taste. There is a wide range of Brazilian coffee. It is not all good but it has a harsher taste than other coffees. Colombian coffee is strong and rich with a slightly bitter taste.

Text (i)
The Chieftain led his charges through the door of the Keep. Then they caught sight of the poet. Sarah rushed to him and slipped a hand inside his shirt to feel the beat of his heart. She raised a cup to his lips.

 *Now turn to the KEY*

2.4 *Non-Verbal Information*

Another important feature of transactional text is that it is often supported by visual information which either restates textual information or provides additional information which is more economically portrayed in a non-verbal way (McEldowney, 1994:11). For instance, we can make use of photographs, drawings, cartoons, diagrams, tables, plans maps, graphs, pie-charts and the like.

Just as there are conventional ways for expressing information verbally so, as pointed by McEldowney (ibid), there are visual conventions related to each of the communicative purposes outlined above.

In the case of instructions there is often a sequence of diagrams each one indicating a step in the instructions. In the case of the recipe in 2.2.1, for instance, the first step might be represented by a hand stirring the ingredients in a bowl and the second by the hand slicing through the butter and the third by hands blending in the ingredients in the bowl and so on

Narratives can also be expressed by a sequence of visuals. In this case, however, the depiction is not so much diagrammatic as pictorial. At the most basic level, each picture in the sequence will show the characters involved and will depict the scene in which the characters find themselves. For, instance with regard to the narrative sequence in 2.2.2, the first picture might show a big fence with a gate in it and a group of heavily armed Chinese people outside, one of whom is banging at the gate and the second a bishop standing just inside the open gate talking to the Chinese and so on. Cartoon strips are also a common method of depicting a sequence of events.

Descriptive information is shown by single illustrative visuals rather than picture sequences of the types just referred to. For instance, with regard to the text about guinea pigs in 2.2.3, the information about raised cages looking like rabbit huts and filled with hay for sleeping in could well be shown in a drawing as could the smooth-haired type of guinea pig. Similarly, small pictures of what the animals eat could be provided by way of illustration.

We note that, just in the way we have indicated a move from more concrete to more abstract, the same is true of the introduction of visual information. For instance a drawing of a room must be familiar before a plan of a room is introduced or a table of figures must precede a graph of some kind.

2.5 ☙ *Try This (3)*

Non-Verbal Information

Study the following 6 pieces of visual material and

(i) *write a simple version of the information depicted by he visual*

(ii) *decide on the communicative purpose of each visual. Write the appropriate letter from the following in the circle provided:*

$$I \quad = instruction$$

$$SD \quad = stative\ description$$

$$NP \quad = \quad description\ of\ natural$$

process

$$MCP \quad = \quad description\ of$$

man-controlled

process

$$N \quad = narration$$

(iii) *indicate the visual conventions that allowed you to recognise the communicative purpose of each visual.*

Visual (2)

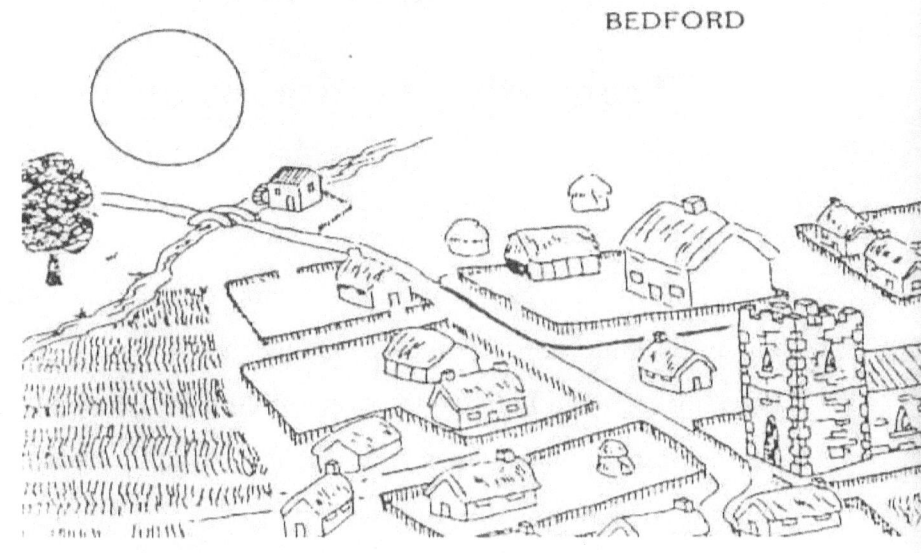
BEDFORD

Chapter Three

Translating Transactional Text

3.1 Introduction

Now that we have an appropriate desciption of transactional text let us examine the hypothesis that the translation of such text does not require a high degree of personal negotiation on the part of the translator and that it is likely to impose a consensus transaltion. Towards this end, we report on a case study in which English transactional text was translated into Arabic by ten people of an adequate standard in both languages in that they were educated Arabic speakers working/studying in the medium of English. The group involved teachers, doctors and researchers. None of them were trained translators.

The group translated Text 4 (2.2.1) a set of instructions for making biscuits; Text 8 (2.2.2) a narration about the Bishop and the Chinese; and Text 12 (2.2.3) a description of the guinea pig. Their translations showed a high level of agreement, a consensus, it is argued, enforced by the nature of the text involved. In many cases, in fact, there was an almost one-to-one correlation between the Arabic and the English on the part of most of the translators. For instance, with regard to the instructions in Text 4 we find:

Mix all the ingedients in the bowl

اخلط جميع المقادير في / وعاء

With regard to narrative:

The Bishop decided to trust them, went to the hospital

and tended to the wounded.

الأسقف قرر (قرر الأسقف) أن يثق بهم،ذهب الى المستشفى و
اعتنى بالجرحى

and with regard to the description:

If cared for, a cavy can live for up to eight years.

إذا أعتني بها ، الكابياء يمكن أن تعيش لمدة ثماني
سنوات

Let us now turn to a more detailed discussion of the results as we consider vocabulary (or word level) translation and grammatical (or system/text level) translation.

3.2   Vocabulary (Word Level Translation)

An examination of the translations with regard to the decoding of words, the smallest units of text, showed that the translators faced few problems arising from lack of equivalence. This is because, in a factual context, it is the propositional meaning of a word that is to be expected. In the instructions for making biscuits (Text 4), for instance, the propositional meaning of a word like sugar is "a sweet crystalline substance obtained from various plants especially sugar cane and sugar beet". This is the type of meaning that can be negotiated to be true or false. One expects a group of competent translators to have no trouble in finding a precise equivalent in Arabic and would expect the whole group to use the same word in their translations. In contrast, in something like 'Come on, Sugar. Let's buy some cake', the word might be translated as "darling", "dear", "love", "sweetheart" or the like. A range of translations is to be expected as individual translators make a choice according to the their experience of the social register in question.

Further, in a piece of transactional text we expect the words used to be related to the same semantic field as determined by the topic written about. Baker (ibid:18) says that these fields reflect the divisions and sub-divisions imposed by a given linguistic community on the continuum of experience. For instance, in Text 4, the words are related to the field of recipes for cooking food and in Text 12 to the care of small animals kept as pets, contexts which are related to areas of universal knowledge clearly common to both the English and Arabic communities. Also, in Text 8, though the events related are specific to a particular time and series of events, the general semantic field is related to another universal - medical help for the wounded in the times of combat of one sort or another. One would not expect translators to have trouble with equivalence as the universal nature of the concepts involved ensures ease of decoding within the given context.

Also, with regard to semantic field, we note that the narrative related in Text 8 makes use of the term armed to the teeth. Only one of the translators actually used the Arabic version of this idiom –مسلحين حتى الأسنان . The others produced a range of glosses for the term, one of which, مسلحين من راسهم حتى قدمهم = armed from head to foot, is like the previous translation, closest to the English. The other glosses - مدججين بالسلاح = heavily armed, مسلحين بالكامل = fully armed, مسلحين بكثرة = armed a lot, على درجة عالية من التسليح = at a high degree of armament, محاربون = fighters are perhaps less exact translations. The central purpose here is, however, not to discuss the best possible translation. The point is that the choices made all communicate the central information and are coherent with the rest of the text. Presumably, the overall transactional meaning restricted the choice of gloss to a degree that might not have been so in a more imaginative context.

In this context, where translators might not know a word like, for instance, cavy, (an animal not familiar in Arab countries) they can use the simple strategy of looking it up in a bi-lingual dictionary. For the reasons referred to above, they are likely to find a dictionary equivalent which will be to the point as was, in fact, the case with regard to cavy. In the event, none of the translators were familiar with the equivalent of cavy in Arabic though a bi-lingual dictionary provided the meaning. Seven used the word. كابياء Two chose to refer to cavy as الخنزير الهندي . Only one was not sure enough any of the above and selected الأرنب البري/wild rabbit. In a different context one referred to cavies as animalsحيوانات . In spite of these slight differences of word choice, however, it can be argued that there was no detrimental loss of information, the particular concept involved being integrated within the general textual concept.

Overall, then, the translators' choice of terms was predominantly appropriate. The terms used were denotative rather than connotative. Bell (ibid:98) explains the difference between denotative and connotative in relation to two aspects of meaning:

> The first refers to meaning which is referential, objective and cognitive and hence, the shared property of the speech community which uses the language of which word or sentence forms a part. The second, in contrast, refers to meaning which is not referential but associational, subjective and affective. This kind of meaning, being personal, may or may not be shared by the community at large

Table One below summarises the 10 attempts made at each word in each of the three texts (Instruction, Narration and Description). They are categorised according to whether the word used by each translator was an "exact translation", an acceptable "variation" or a "mistake".

A word was considered to be an exact translation if it represented a one-to-one equivalent of the English. An "exact translation" can be used to refer to a translated item that plays a constructive role in the achievement of a textual communication. In this respect Beaugrande & Dressler (1981:7) explain that the set of occurences should constitute a cohesive and coherent text instrumantal in fulfilling the producer's intention e.g. to distribute knowledge or attain a goal specified in a plan. Thus, an exact translation can be said to be one that is suitable in a transactional context because it conveys the meaning intended for a particular situation. This was, for instance, the case with regard to مبتدئين beginners. Table One indicates that 45% of the 1160 attempts made to translate a word in the study were, in fact, an exact translation of this type. Synonyms were also considered to be an exact translation as was the case with keep يقتني ،يحتفظ، يربي . Such translations represented 33.3% of the attempts made. This means that, in total, 10 inexperienced translators were able to produce what can be considered an exact translation of the words involved on 78.3% of their attempts.

Table One: Translation Attempts of the Vocabulary Items in the Three Texts

		Instruction (Text 4)		Narration (Text 8)		Description (Text 12)		Totals (all texts)			
		No.	%	No.	%	No.	%	No.	%	No.	%
Exact Translation	Same	204	42.5	121	60.5	197	41.0	522	45.0		
	Synonym	155	32.3	31	15.5	200	41.7	386	33.3	908	7.
Variations	Super-ordinate	19	4.0	2	1.0	9	1.9	30	2.6		
	Explanation	72	1.5	24	12.0	30	6.3	126	10.9		
	Hyponym	1	0.2	-	-	2	0.4	3	0.3	183	1.
	Implicit	13	2.7	4	2.0	7	1.5	24	2.0		

Mistakes	*Wrong Word*	*3*	*0.6*	*14*	*7.0*	*14*	*2.9*	*31*	*2.7*	*69*	*6.0*
	Omission	*13*	*2.7*	*4*	*2.0*	*21*	*4.4*	*38*	*3.3*		
		480		*200*		*480*		*1160*		*1160*	

On Table One above the term "variation" refers to choices which depart slightly from the consensus choice of the study group. It refers to choices which do not block the producer's goal or disturb communication. With regard to items considered to be acceptable variations, problems may arise in translation when the target language fails to provide a direct equivalent for a word in the source text. In Text 4, for instance, the participants could not find a direct equivalent for the word bowl meaning سلطانية. It seems that they did not consider سلطانية as a suitable equivalent for bowl. Seven out of the ten used الوعاء/إناء which means "vessel" or "container"; one used طبق عميق ("deep dish"); one used إناء عميق ("deep vessel") and one used زبدية الخلط ("clay mixing bowl"). We note that وعاء and إناء are general in reference or super-ordinate (their meaning implying or including that of another) while زبدية الخلط العميقة are more specific or hyponyms. Extreme specification is not necessary to maintain the original meaning in that utensil or container are both quite adequate to express the meaning in the given context. It may be that the participants resorted to a super-ordinate term or chose to explain the term with الطبق العميق ("deep dish") because سلطانية is not very common in many Arab countries.

For sticky (Text 4), seven out of the ten participants used لزج. One, however, used متماسك ("cohesive", "in close contact") instead of لزج another used متلاصق ("sticking together") and a third used متجانس ("having the same structure or nature"). In this last case the translator added some further information to explain what the mixture should be like – that is, not only sticky but the ingredients should be well mixed together.

In Text 4 seven participants translated light brown as بني فاتح ("light brown") or بني ("brown"). Another participant used ذهبي ("gold"), apparently using previous knowledge as to how biscuits should be. Two, however, used يتحمر ("become reddish") which in Arabic is used to describe something baked or even grilled. It seems that these two chose a culture-specific term to transfer a meaning unlike that in the source language.

With regard to work surface, the Arabic translations showed various equivalents. The assumption is that the Arabic is a direct super-ordinate or hyponym. The nearest super-ordinate used was الطاولة ("table"). It was explained as being a particular type of table – طاولة العمل ("a work table"). Others translated the term as اللوح الخشبي ("the wooden board") or مكان التحضير

("the preparation place"), more of a generalisation. Resorting to such a generalisation is a common strategy in translation, particularly in texts where propositional meaning is dominant, and here it has little affect with regard to the communication of the steps of the recipe.

Such variations, categorised as "super-ordinate", "explanation" and "hyponym", and which are not considered to represent a loss in meaning occurred on 11.8% of occasions (Table One). On a further 2% of occasions meaning was implied in the text rather than being represented by another word. For instance, in Use the knife to cut up the <u>butter</u>, then knead with your fingers until the flour and sugar are blended into the <u>butter</u> and the mixture is sticky, the word butter is used twice. In the Arabic, however, the word is used only once and the second time it is implied تقطع الزبدة بالسكين ثم تفرك بالأصابع مع الدقيق و السكرحتى يصبح المزيج لزجا. ("The butter is cut by the knife, then is kneaded with fingers with flour and sugar until the mixture is sticky"). Another example occurs with regard to touch in the sentence Make sure that their edges do not <u>touch.</u> Two of the participants implied the meaning مع مراعاة ترك مسافات - ("take into consideration leaving spaces") and بحيث تكون كل بسكويتة بعيدة عن الأخرى ("such that every biscuit is far from the other").

This means that 15.8% of the total attempts at translating words might be considered variations from the original but they did not represent a loss in meaning.

With very few exceptions of the type related above the majority of translations used almost the same words. Those who deviated made only a slight negotiation with regard to meaning, a negotiation often related to personal knowledge of the subject. Such deviations, however, did not distort the source texts and seem to be the result in the transactional field of what Hasan (1985:71) refers to when she says that the texture of a text is manifested by certain kinds of semantic relations.

Before leaving this point about the ease of translating lexis in a transactional context, we note that, of the 1160 possible attempts, only 6% represented what could be considered as mistakes. A "mistake" was considered to have occurred when a word or expression failed to touch on what was intended by the producer of the source text. The mistake may have been the result of misunderstanding or lack of knowledge. The small number of mistakes evidenced by the study seems remarkable given that the subjects of the study were not trained and experienced translators. Further, of this 6%, 3.3% were errors of "omission" where the translator, perhaps not familiar with a word like hardy, for instance, simply ignored it. In fact, this figure is in reality even smaller when we see that, among the 38 occurrences recorded, twelve of these are the result of two translators leaving out the last sentences of Text 12 and the last sentence of Text 4 presumably because of time pressure. Only 31 attempts (2.7%) resulted in the use of what might be considered a "wrong word". For instance, in Text 12 the word cage is translated as كهف ("cave").

As well as looking at how lexis was translated we need to investigate what happened with regard to the grammatical system of the source text.

3.3 The Grammatical System (Text Level Translation)

As we have seen the communicative purpose in both source and target language is marked by a cluster of conventional grammatical features. Knowledge of these allows for the transference from one language to the other to be carried out in a systematic manner.

Differences in grammatical detail in the source and target languages might lead to some alteration in message content during the process of translation. This might take the form of the addition of information which is not in the source text. For instance, in Arabic gender is marked systematically in a way it is not in English. In English, for instance, the instruction word Mix is used to address both male and female with no grammatical marking. In Arabic, however, transactional instructions are normally given in the masculine (اخلط، استعمل، افرك،اخبز) unless a female is being addressed directly. Two of the participants used the feminine form in translation – ،اخلطي/ /ادلقي، افردي، ضعي. The other translators used the masculine, functioning as the dominant or unmarked term used where the sex of the addressee is not known. When the female translator was questioned about her choice to use the feminine form she explained that she had provided information for the makers of biscuits – in Arab countries it is the women who do most of the cooking.

The point to stress here, however, is that the translator should be aware of the two different grammatical systems so that the transfer between two transactional texts should be relatively straightforward. With an awareness of the broad framework of form outlined in Chapter Two with regard to transactional examples of instruction, narrating and describing, there should, however, be no need for the competent translator to add to or to lose information from the source text in the move from one set of grammatical markers to the other and, on the whole, this proved to be the case with regard to the translations produced in the case study.

As indicated in 2.1.1 above with regard to the Arab recipe, we saw that instructions are typically expressed in Arabic with a sequence of imperative forms relating to the sequence of steps to be carried out. Thus, in Text 4, the English instructions using the dynamic stem forms mix, use, knead, tip, flatten, etc to indicate a series of steps to be carried out in the making of biscuits can be expressed in Arabic by ،اخلط، استعمل، اعجن/

افرد، افرغ/ also imperative forms showing no inflection. We note that eight of the ten participants systematically used imperative forms throughout their translation, thus indicating no problem in moving at this basic transactional level from one language system to the other.

In addition, the English convention of adding warnings and comments to aid the reader in the process of following a set of instructions was closely adhered to by the translators who used the imperative form. For instance, all translated you may need as ربما تحتاج and make sure as تأكد من عدم .

Two of the translators, however, chose to use passive forms rather than imperatives in their translation of the recipe and, for instance, we find the Arabic sequence تُمزج، تُقطع، تُفرك، يُنثر، يُقسم، يوضع،تُخبز، تُرفع، توضع . In this respect, we note that, beside the normal convention of couching recipes in instructional terms, in English less commonly passive forms may occur. For instance, All the ingredients are mixed in the bowl. The knife is used to cut up the butter which is then kneaded with the fingers .... Here, according to McEldowney (1990), the communicative purpose is strictly one way of describing the process of making biscuits rather than that of giving the reader instructions for carrying out the steps involved. The result is a rather more impersonal approach to recipe information. It is this convention that has been picked up by the two translators involved. They have communicated the essential information of the original but in a more formal style than that indicated by the original Text 4. This formality is maintained by the translation of You may need to put flour on the work surface, a tip addressed directly to the reader, by the impersonal قد تحتاج الى رش الدقيق على سطح العمل ("You might need to sprinkle flour on the work surface") and يرش الدقيق ("Flour is to be sprinkled on the work surface ").

Though the departure from the instructions of the original text to a description of the process represented by the use of passive forms marks a shift from the style of the source text, it adheres to an English convention with regard to transactional language. One of the translators, however, departed from the English convention by adhering to the Arabic way of ending a recipe by wishing her addressees "enjoyment and good health" (وبالهناء والعافية). The same translator also intervened by adding an extra piece of advice on taking the biscuits out of the oven – (تركيها حتى تبرد)("Leave it to cool"). Similarly, another translator rendered to keep the mixture from sticking as حتى تسهل عملية نقل البسكويت إلى صينية الفرن ("to move to the oven tray in easily") in explanation of why flour should be used to keep the mixture from sticking. It is to be noted that such interference/negotiation on the part of the translators was very rare indeed and grammatical negotiation was as rare as that indicated above with regard to vocabulary.

As indicated above, the overall coherence of the instruction text was maintained by all the translators in that they used a set of either imperative or passive forms in a consistent manner and did not mix masculine and feminine forms. Further, as we saw in 2.1.1, the sequence of occurrence which adds coherence to instructional texts is the same in both languages and was adhered to by all of the translators involved in the case study.

As with the recipe in Text 4, the narrative outlined in Text 8 is given a central coherence by a sequence of events. In this case, however, the sequence of occurrence is one expressed by a series of events said to have been carried out on a particular occasion when a Chinese deputation approached a bishop to get help for their injured colleagues. The events are related by a series of verbs in the past tense – arrived, begged, decided, went, tended expressed in the order in which the events happened.

As we saw above in 1.7 such a straightforward outlining of events does not necessarily occur in literary narrative. Various effects are created by tinkering with the order in which events are related according to personal preference and, as will be discussed later, this tinkering leads to a great deal of negotiation when it comes to translation. In this case, with regard to the transactional Text 8, the Arabic versions all maintained the coherence of the sequence of events and used a sequence of past verbs, the conventional form for the expression of a narrative sequence in Arabic just as it is in English – وصل، كان، ذهب، قرر .

In the English narrative, the verbs are preceded by "doer(s)" of the action in the form of the sentence subject. As we saw in Chapter Two, however, the conventional word order is different. The Arabic uses verbal sentences of the forms VSO وصل وفد غريب إلى مجمع المفوضية or VOS كان معهم بعض الأدوية. The translators had no problems in systematically applying Arabic sentence conventions as they moved from the English source text to their Arabic translation.

As indicated in Chapter Two, narrative events often have a descriptive introduction and conclusion and further descriptive comments occur within the sequence of events for a wide range of different purposes – to set the scene, to provide the reasons for or results of events, to comment on the appearance, motives, character of the doers of the events and so on. In the source text we find the descriptive sentences They were Chinese armed to the teeth, on a mission of mercy. They knew the Bishop had some medicines. These two sentences occur immediately following the first step in the narrative (.... a strange deputation arrived at the mission compound) with the purpose of explaining who the deputation were and why they were there. Though the position in which description might occur within a transactional narrative sequence is relatively less fixed than the order in which events are related, it is more likely to occur in close spatial association to the event to which it is related. Here, it is purely the position of occurrence, each sentence introduced by they, which indicates the relationship of the descriptive comments to the initial narrative step. This positioning of the descriptive sentences was adhered to by all the translators in the case study.

Most often in Arabic description the equivalent of the verb 'to be' is omitted in the present tense. It appears, however, in past description. For instance, They are Chinese might be expressed هم صينيون ("They Chinese"). Here, however, all the translations used the "were" form – كانوا صينيين. Moreover, with regard to the English descriptive sentence without 'be' – They knew the Bishop had some medicines, all ten translations inserted were كانوا يعلمون أن الأسقف يملك بعض الأدوية ("Were they knew the Bishop"; "They were knew the Bishop"). It is used here to assert the fact that the Bishop had some medicines as well as the past tense concept. It is used in a way similar to the past perfect tense.

The English Text 12 is a general description of the care of guinea pigs kept as pets. In this context, as seen in Chapter Two, the present tense verbs is, are, like, eat, can crop and so on are stative and coherence is given to the information not by a sequence of actions but by a conceptual grouping. In Arabic the convention is also to use the present tense but the use of the verb BE, a common feature of English, is not normal in Arabic. The translators used the appropriate Arabic verb convention. Some translators implied the verb BE again by asserting the identity of cavy using pronominal reference الإسم الحقيقي لخنزير غينيا هو الكابياء - The correct name for guinea pig (he) a cavy.

In English, sentences with 'be' are of the SVC form. In Arabic, such information is related in nominal sentences in which the form is SO or SC – for instance, الأسم الصحيح لخنزير غينيا هو الكابياء. Where the verb is not 'be' in English, sentences maintain a similar word order SVO or SVC. In Arabic such a sentence can be verbal تحب الكابياء الأقفاص المرتفعة ("Like cavies raised cages") or nominal الكابياء تحب الأقفاص المرتفعة ("Cavies like raised cages") – word order is more flexible in Arabic. Translators moved comfortably from one grammatical system to the other in this respect, the differences not resulting in any change in information suggesting that, when in control of two systems of transactional communication, translators can move backwards and forwards with comparative ease.

Coherence in both the source text and the translations is achieved in the same way. The translators followed the order in which the source text expressed the descriptive concepts involved, moving from name and type through the elements of care related to living conditions, food and water and ending with a comment about life span.

Inserted in the description of the source text are two warnings in the form of instructions. They logically follow the expression of the concepts they are related to. For instance, but enclose and protect them follows the descriptive comment that they may be let out into the garden in summer and but do not let them get fat follows the comment that they like hot bran in winter in addition to their normal diet. Seven of the ten translators, using the equivalent instructional form, included these warnings at the same point as in the English text thus adhering to the English convention.

The insertion of these warnings, however, led to certain deviations on the part of the other three participants in the case study. One completely ignored the first warning and another the second. This was probably merely due to negligence on the part of the translators involved. One translator, however, changed the tone of the first warning about protection in the garden rendering it لذا يفضل أن تبقى عليهم في القفص لحمايتهم ("therefore, it is safer to keep them in the cage for their protection"). Perhaps influenced by the inclusion of these warnings in the original, some translators made stronger the descriptive comment They need plenty of water, changed each day, from large water bottles by the use of "should" and by describing the water as "clean"– تحتاج الكابياء الى الكثير من الماء النظيف الذي يجب تجديده كل يوم.

Thus, at text level, a knowledge of the broad grammatical framework of both languages involved in translation ensured that the translators, having recognised the textual continuity of a source text, were, on the whole, able to produce a text in the target language which demonstrated the textual coherence typical of that language. Because of this, each of the ten translations of the study "hang together" appropriately. The result is a text that will enable the reader to make biscuits, or care for a guinea pig as a pet or understand the situation with regard to the Chinese deputation. The translations are to the point and homogeneous in form. Negotiation is minimal. The main variations from the original tend to represent a slight shift in style with two translators producing a more formal set of instructions and one translator producing a slightly more prescriptive comment with regard to the care of guinea pigs. The other type of deviation was to do with the insertion of additional information on as few as two or three occasions. In one case this was to do with the imposition of the Arabic convention of wishing her readers well and in the others the translator added a little personal touch to help the reader. It might be that these minimal negotiations are to do with the fact that the participants in the study are not trained translators. The fact remains that, despite their relative lack of experience and training in the skill of translation, all the participants had very little problem in dealing with the translation of the transactional texts.

According to Baker (1992:173) a translator cannot always follow the thematic organisation of the original. She believes that this is because syntactic features like restrictions on word order, the principle of end-weight and the natural phraseology of the target language may intervene. As we have seen, however, this did not seem to be a problem with regard to transactional texts. The more restricted code of a sequence of events took care of the thematic organisation of the instructions and narrative and the conceptual organisation of the description was followed with ease.

Within the broad organisational framework represented by sequential and conceptual control of McEldowney's model we note, however, Newmark's comment that the topic of cohesion has always appeared to me the most useful constituent of discourse analysis or text linguistics applicable to translation (1987:295). Here, the reference is to the network of lexical, grammatical and other relations which provide links between parts of text (Baker, 1992:180). In this respect, Halliday & Hasan (1985) outline the five main cohesive devices of English as reference, substitution, ellipsis, conjunction and lexical cohesion.

In our texts the device of reference, for instance, is illustrated by the pronominal use in Use the cutter to make biscuits and lay them on the baking tray. Make sure their edges do not touch in which them and their refer back to biscuits. A similar continuity of reference occurs in the narrative with regard to the underlined forms in ..a strange deputation arrived at the mission compound. They were armed to the teeth. They were Chinese.....They knew the bishop had some medicines and they begged him to go with them to the hospital. With regard to this last example, for instance, we see that in a transactional context the Arabic is closer to the English pattern – وصل وفد غريب/كانوا يعرفون أن المطران يمتلك بعض الأدوية / توسلوا اليه) ("arrived a strange deputation / were they knew the Bishop had some medicine / they begged him"). The chain of reference in Arabic is achieved in almost the same way as in the English.

We note, however, that there is perhaps a shift in emphasis in Arabic with regard to pronominal reference. In the last example, where English refers back to the Bishop with him, the Arabic translator repeats the Bishop. In Arabic it is sometimes preferable to use names rather than pronouns to trace participants back through discourse, perhaps because of the length of Arabic sentences. In this respect, in the description text in English we note the occurrence of The correct name for <u>guinea pig</u> is <u>cavy</u>. The more hardy smooth-haired <u>kinds</u> are .. <u>Cavies</u> like raised cages... <u>They</u> eat little and often. This is then followed by alternating examples of they and them and finally ..... <u>a cavy</u> can live for up to eight years. The word cavy is repeated at the end to draw the paragraph to a close but the network of reference is largely pronominal. In contrast, the translators repeated the term a great deal more often than the English original. Of the translators,

1 used the word 3 times

1 used the word 4 times

2 used the word 5 times

3 used the word 6 times

1 used the word 8 times

1 used the word 9 times.

That is, on the average the word was repeated 5.2 times indicating that Arabic seems to favour lexical repetition for cohesive reference as a means of reducing ambiguity with regard to tracing participants through a text.

Another difference with regard to the two languages is that Arabic is more inflected than English and there is thus greater marking of the relationship between participants and processes and actions. For instance, in the English The more hardy smooth-haired kinds are best for beginners to keep, as indicated above, kinds is used to refer back to cavy (and guinea pig) in the first sentence. This is an example of ellipsis in which kinds stands for kinds of guinea pig. Further, the agreement of verbs with their subjects in gender and number must be marked in Arabic though this is not a central feature of English.

It remains, however, that the finer details of grammatical convention of the type just illustrated with regard to reference and ellipsis and those referred to above with regard to sentence order have no real effect on the communication of the basic information of a transactional text as a translator competent in the structure of both languages moves from English to Arabic.

3.4   Conclusion

The Arabic translations of the study show a high degree of homogeneity. They are all coherent according to the conventions of Arabic, but, because of the transactional nature of the text involved, also show a very close match with the English source texts both with regard to lexis and structure. In fact, as illustrated in 3.1 above, there are sections of text in Arabic which are almost one-to-one equivalents of the English.

The degree of uniqueness depends on the individual translator involved and, as we shall see later, we may expect a great deal of personal variation when it comes to the translation of more literary texts. Halliday (1985:42) says, in this respect,

> Some texts are indeed highly valued for their uniqueness; it is this property we have in mind when we say that something belongs to the rather vaguely defined category of "literature". A literary text is a text that is valued in its own right, which must mean that it differs from all other texts.

In transactional texts of the type we have used in the study, the amount of extraneous information that needs to be restored by the translator in the target text is slight. Little has to be implied. A translator who encounters some type of "untranslatability" in that there is no adequate equivalence in the target may, however, need to resort to implication. In this respect Catford (1965) distinguishes two types of untranslatability which he terms "linguistic" and "cultural". Linguistic examples, as indicated above in 3.2, for instance, perhaps with regard to bowl (at the word level), occur when a translator cannot find a lexical or syntactic item in the target language for an item in the source language. The factual nature and universality of the concepts involved in the texts of our study meant, however, that translators were able to provide a suitable factual gloss for such examples and had no need to enrich or clarify the source language text during the translation process. A syntactic example of untranslatability can be seen with regard to There has been an accident and Ther was an accident. The second sentence can be translated into Arabic كات هناك حادث Whereas the first cannot be rendered adequately in structural terms without adding an explanation to express the recent and continuous effect of the present perfect tense- كان هناك حادث قبل قليل/منذ فترة وجيزة

Cultural untranslatability is due to the lack of relevant situation in the culture of the target language. It is concerned with prior knowledge of the world. Where, for instance, a translator addressed the instructions of Text 4 to a female rather than a universal audience, we see the use of her awareness that, in her culture, recipes are usually addressed to females. Her translation did not convey the impersonal style of the source text, a style typical of recipes written in English.

Chapter Four

Learning to Translate Transactional Text

4.1 Some Initial Considerations

4.1.1 The Basis for Learning

As was indicated in Chapter One, transactional language has an important role to play in education and in life in general. Across the curriculum, it is the language of the classroom, the language of textbooks and the language of examinations. Further, as pointed out by McEldowney (1994:3), it is the type of language by which the community at large conducts day-to-day business. Thus, both the academic progress and the life style of an individual who cannot control this type of language will be seriously impeded. As a result, the student of translation must be in control of a transactional style in both languages .

As well as the need to control transactional style for the reasons just referred to, because of its relatively straightforward nature, which, as we have seen, allows for consensus translation, it represents an obvious starting point for the learning of translation. As argued by McEldowney (ibid), transactional language provides the basis for learning the other forms of language referred to in Chapter One as "social language" and "literary language". Similarly, the translator who is in control of a transactional style can use it as the tool for moving onto greater complexities of language including the social and literary conventions of the two languages involved in the process, in this case, English and Arabic.

4.1.2   Language Learning and Translation

The aim of teaching translation is to ensure that the learner acquires two interrelated skills – the skill of communicating effectively in the particular languages involved as well as the skill of effectively transferring information from one language to another. From this standpoint it can be argued that, initially, learning how to translate can best follow the same route as learning a new language.In the early stages the two can most effectively be entwined. At later stages, the two processes will divert and move along somewhat separate paths.

4.1.3   Learning and Communication

In coding and decoding messages in their own language people use, without conscious thought, a complex linguistic code. Language and translation teachers must have an awareness of the system involved if they are to guide their learners to master another language and use it to translate messages encoded in that language. This linguistic awareness is necessary to enable learners to become independent communicators as rapidly as possible (McEldowney, 1990:28).

Further, human communication is characterised by a natural desire for information. In this context content is a crucial element in learning and demonstrating the knowledge of the code involved in the communication of messages. If there is no information to work with there is no means of manipulating and, therefore learning, the linguistic code involved. Thus, both language learner and the trainee translator can best begin with a source or input text to process. This innate interest in knowledge can be used to drive learners on to accumulate as well as impart knowledge to others. Thus, exposure to factual content can be used early on as the trigger which activates the learner.

4.1.4 *Textuality*

It is implicit in what we have just said and in our identification of the features of the communicative purposes of transactional language that it is the way a whole piece of text hangs together which is important. Beaugrande and Dressler (1980:13, 35) as well as Halliday (1985: 4-6,48) seem to agree that language should be viewed as a system which is a *set of elements each of which has a function of contributory to the workings of the whole or a set of elements functioning together.*

When considering a piece of text from the point of view of the reader, Beaugrande (1980:35) proposes that *the text itself be viewed as a system* and this view is repeated by Halliday (1985:48) who says that every text provides *a context for itself.* He says that a text hangs together as a result of its internal coherence which comes about from *the set of linguistic resources that every language has for linking one part of a text to another.*

He stresses the importance of the reader's *internal expectations* in maintaining the flow and understanding of text. He has in mind the work of the anthropologist Brinslaw Malinowski (1923, 1935) and his theory of the context of situation.

To a large extent, it is the degree of familiarity with the way a text is put together that determines the ease and manner of discovering its meaning. As we have seen, where emphasis is on real-world meaning and information has been imparted in a systematic and predictable way, readers have a relatively straightforward task. They are able to bring their experience of world knowledge and their experience of similar text to bear in extracting the information involved. In conveying fact, the writer does not *present information in a very difficult and ambiguous form* .. nor *force the reader to revise expectation* (Beaugrande, 1978:47). Most readers will decode the same basic information and most translators will pass it on with little distortion.

4.2   Methodology

Taking account of the points made above the aim here is to illustrate a way in which to equip the trainee translator with the listening and reading skills necessary for independent acquisition of information from a wide range of appropriate English sources and with the speaking and writing skills necessary for the expression and discussion of this information and the ability to pass it on in another language.

Pedagogically, it is assumed that content should be used to provide a mental need for interaction employing appropriate language structures. In language learning the aim is to achieve a direct shift from input to output information in the same language without the use of intermediaries of any kind while that of translation is to achieve a similar shift from one language to another. Towards such an end, learners need to build up an adequate store of linguistic and real-world information. This can be achieved through a process of working through listening and reading material from a wide range of sources and, as they go, learners need constantly to practise recycling information by initiating their own communication from information received in the target language (McEldowney, 1990:13).

In the classroom the process of recycling just referred to can be facilitated by two main integrated activities with regard to a source or input text:

- working towards the discovery of the meaning of vocabulary items in context
- using a catalyst of summary notes that distil the linguistic forms and arrangement of concepts in such a way as to highlight normal textual cohesion and coherence

4.2.1 *Vocabulary*

Learners should be trained to realise that they do not need to "know" the meaning of each individual word in a text before they can understand, and indeed translate, an overall message. They must develop an awareness that it is possible to infer a great deal from a given context. In Text 4, for instance, a reader might not be familiar with the word ingredients. Nevertheless there are code markers which enable those familiar with them to make a start on the road to discovery. In Mix all the ingredients in the bowl, we note that all, the and –s indicate ingredients to be the name of something. This is reinforced by its position as the object of the verb mix. As McEldowney (1996/7:18) says, there are items within the language code which tell us what words refer to on any one occasion, items that tell us whether they refer to "things", "qualities", "actions" and the like and that it is through the exercise of such awareness that learners are helped towards the goal of becoming effective language learners. Further, in

Text 4, within the general context of a recipe, there are many indications that go on to clarify the meaning of the term. For instance, the field of meaning indicated by mix and in a bowl suggest items that can be blended together as the basis of something. Then, reference to butter, flour and sugar in what seems to be an explanation of the first sentence suggest that these are related to ingredients, marked as they are in each case by an anaphoric the. This is further reinforced by the fact that these parts are blended into a whole referred to as the mixture, again with the use of anaphoric the. The ingredients have been listed as butter, flour and sugar and mixed together to form a whole.

In transactional language, in which meaning is relatively concrete and predictable, learners can be led to infer meaning through tasks which lead them to recognise the signposts represented by the linguistic markers involved at the same time as they build up an awareness of how the language works in this respect.

Such awareness of how meaning works can be integrated into work with textual summaries of the type developed throughout her writings by McEldowney and referred to by her as "transition notes".

4.2.2   Transition Notes

Transition notes represent a distillation of the linguistic features and discourse organisation of a given text (McEldowney, 1990:24). They guide the learners cognitively as well as linguistically. Initially, guided comprehension tasks help learners to make notes from a source text. As learning progresses the control becomes less and less until learners can make their own notes without help. Once notes have been developed they become the basis for the learner's output both spoken and *written.*

Let us now see what transition notes for Texts 4, 8 and 12 might look like for what might be considered an intermediate level of learning.

4.2.2.1 Instruction

Mix	*your ingredients*	*in a bowl*	
Cut up	*the butter*		*with a knife*
Blend	*the flour & sugar*	*into the butter*	*with your fingers*
Put	*some flour*	*on the work surface*	
Tip out	*the mixture*		
Flatten	*it*		
Make	*some biscuits*		*with a cutter*
Lay	*them*	*on a baking tray*	
Set	*the oven*		*to Gas Mark 4*
Bake	*the biscuits*		*for 20 minutes*
Take	*them*	*out of the oven*	*with a cloth*
Place	*the tray*	*on a board*	

In the first column we note the sequence of steps involved represented by the stem (imperative) form of the verb. The second column represents "what" or the sentence object. The remaining columns represent adverbial elements of one type or another. Depending on the level of the learner, the adverbials might all be listed on one column or, as here, each type of adverbial might have its own column – "where", "instrument", "limit", "duration". Reading down the notes reveals the main sequence of steps involved. This indicates the overall coherence of the text. Reading across reveals the elements in each sentence – VO, VOA or VOAA. The amount of detail included in the notes will depend on the level of the learners as is indicated in the following section.

Such notes allow for the control of the rather complex web of determiner and pronominal reference in English, something which we saw in Chapter 3 is somewhat different in Arabic. In the notes above we note that first reference is marked, as appropriate, by your, a or some. Reference back is then marked by the. It and them refer back to singular and plural referents respectively.

A reconstruction of the notes might produce a version of the original information something like:

> Mix your ingredients in a bowl. Cut up the butter with a knife. Blend the flour and sugar into the butter with your fingers. Put some flour on the work surface. Tip out the mixture. Flatten it ....[4]

4.2.2.2 ✍ Try This (4)

Transition Notes: Instruction

1. Look at Text (j) below and list the steps in the order they are to be carried out. See if you can identify 10 steps.

---

[4] This simpler version has implications for syllabus design as discussed below in 4.3

(Text J)
Use only three heaped dessertspoonfuls to a pint of water. Do not use the normal four.

Measure the coffee into a warmed jug. Add the correct amount of boiling water and stir it well. Let it stand for a minute and draw the edge of a spoon across the top. Leave the pot for another four minutes – somewhere warm produces the best results. Strain and serve.

➔ Now turn to the **KEY**.

2. From information in Text (j),

(i) list the "whats" after each step - 1. Warm   a jug

(ii) add 3 necessary "wheres" in a third column

(iii) add 2 "how longs" in a fourth column

➔ Now turn to the **KEY**.

3. Look at columns two, three and four of your notes and

(i)   circle items mentioned for the first time

(ii)   underline items which are mentioned for a second time

(iii)   draw an arrow to show the relationships

For instance,

| 1 | Warm | a jug | |
| 2 | Measure | some coffee | into the jug |

(iv)   Describe the system of cohesion illustrated by the notes.

➔ Now turn to the **KEY**.

4. From the notes write a simple reconstruction. Begin
Warm a jug. Measure some coffee into the jug.
→ Now turn to the **KEY**.

5. Make notes to show the steps in making a candle clock
from information in Text (k).

Text (k)
*Hammer two nails through a piece of wood and turn the
wood over so that the points are sticking up. Take two
candles about five inches long and push a candle down on
each nail. Place a watch near the candles and light one of
them. Wait for five minutes and paint a line on the other
candle to mark the height of the burning candle. Wait
another five minutes and repeat the procedure. Continue
until the first candle is burned away. Each line represents
five minutes. You have made a candle clock.*

→ *Now turn to the KEY.*

4.2.2.3 Narration

Text 8 also centres around a sequence of events and thus would
also be controlled by a column of dynamic verbs in the
appropriate form.

Some Chinese	*arrived*		*at* the
mission	*at dawn*		
They	*asked* the bishop	*to go with them*	
He	*went*		*to the hospital* with
them			
He	*tended*	*the wounded*	

Here, as with the instructions, the sequence is revealed on the y-axis and individual sentence structure on the x-axis. Referential usage is controlled in the way suggested with regard to Text 4. A reconstruction from them might be:

> Some Chinese arrived at the mission at dawn. They asked the bishop to go with them. He went to the hospital with them. He tended the wounded

If descriptive information were to be added, the notes might look like this:

Some Chinese arrived   *at the mission*   *at*
dawn   *[armed]*
They   *asked*   *the bishop*   *to go with them*
       [some medicines]
He   *went*   *to*   *the*
hospital   *with them*
He   *tended*   *the wounded*
      [fourteen Chinese]

We note that in the case of description the verbs do not carry the central meaning in the way of instructive and narrative sequence. For this reason the notes pick out the central concept words. Reconstructing these notes would produce something like Some Chinese arrived at the mission at dawn. **They were armed.** They asked the bishop to go with them. **He had some medicines** and so on.

4.2.2.4 📠 *Try This (5)*

Transition Notes: Narration

1.   Look at Text (l) below and:

(i)   list the steps in the order they were carried out

(ii)   add a "what" column and then a "where" column

(iii)   include a "who" column for the doer of the actions in front of the steps

(iv)   check your determiner/pronoun usage and describe the

system

(v)   from your notes write a simple reconstruction of the

narrative sequence

(vi)   add a descriptive column to your notes

(vii)   from your notes reconstruct the narrative with description included

Text (l)

Vernon arrived home from work later than usual and made a jug of coffee. He was tired and tense after the events of the day. He poured out a mugful and sat down to enjoy it. He took a sip. It was strong and bitter just the way he liked it. He smiled and began to relax and the various trials of the day receded into the background.

➔ Now turn to the **KEY**.

2.   Look at Text (m) and make notes to show the sequence of steps involved in Bonnet's experiment. Add a column for description.

Text (m)
Bonnet was a French biologist who experimented with insect communication. In one experiment he placed a large flower swarming with ants on one end of a table. He then put a pile of sugar at the other end. The ants moved backwards and forwards between the two. Then Bonnet drew his finger across the trail. This caused great confusion and the ants began to move out sideways. Presently some of the foragers on one side of the finger trail recognised those on the other side. They then reconnected their trail. From this Bonnet concluded that ants follow a scent trail.

➔ Now turn to the **KEY**.

4.2.2.5 Stative Description

In the case of Text 12, a stative description, the notes would similarly centre around the concepts expressed rather than around a sequence of verbs. That is, information is tabulated rather than providing what is basically a flow chart of events. If the bulk of the information is retrieved, the tabulation would perhaps have three columns:

Guinea Pigs

	Name	*cavies*
General	**Purpose**	*pets*
	Suitable Type	*hardy smooth-haired*
Living Conditions	**Suitable Cages**	*raised hay*

Care	**Feeding**	*little* *often*
	Basic Food	*carrots, turnips* *apple peel* *bread* *a special mix*
	Summer Food	*grass*
	Winter Food	*bran*
	Water	*plenty* *fresh*
Life Expectancy		*8 years*

The information in each cell allows for the reconstruction of an appropriate descriptive sentence - Guinea pigs are called cavies. They make pets. A suitable type is hardy and smooth-haired. Suitable cages are raised They should contain hay. They eat little and often and so on.

The table indicates that textual coherence revolves around conceptual organisation. Hence, all the information about care related to food and water is grouped together. We note that, compared to a text arranged around a sequnce of occurrence the writer has greater choice with regard to overall information. Here, we have general information followed by that to do with details of caring ending with a comment about life expectancy, presumably as a result of good care.

We note that further columns could be added to such a table for further practice. So, for instance, another column might be headed *rabbits* and another *gerbils*. Learners would then need to carry out a library search to complete each cell with appropriate information.

4.2.2.6 ☙ *Try This (6)*

Transition Notes: Stative Description

1. *Read Text (n) and make transition notes by following the tasks below it.*

Text (n)
Keswick Castle is of the motte and bailey type. It has two parts.

The motte is a small hill, circular in shape. It is surrounded by a deep ditch. On the top is a wooden tower.

To the south of the motte is a piece of flat land, a field. This is the bailey which is circular in shape and covers about three times the area of the motte. It also has a ditch around it. On the inside of the dtich is an earth bank with a row of wooden posts along the top forming a stockade. Inside the bailey stockade are several buildings. The square one in the middle is the soldiers' living quarters. The small square building to the north of this is the chapel. The long buildings are store houses.

(i)   Read the first paragraph and
- find out how many parts
- find their names

(ii)   Read the second paragraph and

- identify 5 pieces of information about the motte

→ Now turn to the **KEY**.

(iii)   Complete the following grid from information in the second
paragraph:

"Appearance"

The Motte	The Bailey
a hill	
small	
circular	
x	

 *Now turn to the KEY.*

(iv)   Complete the following from the third paragraph:

"Defences"

The Motte		The Bailey	
a ditch	*around the motte*		

→ Now turn to the **KEY**.

(v)   Tabulate the information about the buildings in the motte

and the bailey. Include only information about position and shape.

→ Now turn to the **KEY**.

(vi)   Put all the information together to make a single table of the

information in Text (n).

(vii)   Use your table to write a simple reconstruction of the text.

→ Now turn to the **KEY**.

2.   Make transition notes of Text (o) below:

Text (o)
There are many different types of coffee. They have different flavours. The coffees of Africa have a strong flavour. They are often very bitter. Blue mountain coffee comes from Jamaica. It is a mixture of coffees and has an unusual taste. There is a wide range of Brazilian coffee which has a harsher taste than other coffees though it is not all good. Colombian coffee is strong and rich with a slightly bitter taste.

→ Now turn to the **KEY**.

4.2.2.7 🐌 *Try This (7)*

Transition Notes: Mixed Communicative Purposes

For Texts (p) to (s) below,

      (i)   decide on the communicative purpose

      (ii)   make appropriate transition notes

      (iii)   write a simple reconstruction from each set of notes

Text (p)
Lumbering is one of the most important occupations in the conifer forests of Canada. Preparations are made in late summer. Most of the timber is felled in winter and transported to the mills in spring.

First suitable trees are selected for felling and camp sites are built through the forest to the water ways. As in Scandinavia, the foresters use the complex system of water ways to transport the timber to the mills. Next, in October, trees are felled by axe and power saw. Then the tops and side branches are cut off to make the enormous trunks easier to handle. This work continues into winter.

When the snow is thick enough, the logs are dragged over the snow by tractor. They are piled onto the ice of the rivers and lakes. Spring comes about mid-April when the snow melts and the logs are floated downstrem to the mills. On arrival they are sorted, while still afloat, into various grades according to species and size. Suitable logs are fed ino the saw mill where they are cut into planks. Other logs have different destinations.

Text (q)
Normally the water cycle consists of five main steps. First, moisture falls on the land either in the form of rain or snow. It then flows into streams and rivers. Water from the rivers goes to the sea from where there is no exit except by evaporation. The cycle is then completed by water falling on the land again.

The Caspian Sea shows an unusual variation of this pattern. Water enters the Caspian in the normal way through three major rivers in the north. Then, each year, a volume of 2 cubic miles flows into the desert where it fills a small depression called the Kara Gulf. This is an enormous evaporation pan dried by sun and wind.

Text (r)
The most important antiquities at Cumae are cut into the hills of the town. High on the west coast are the caves of the Sybil. In the caves a long corridor is cut through the

rocks in a straight north-south line. It continues south from the entrance for 427 feet.

The floor of the corridor is a little less than eight feet wide. The flat ceiling is four feet wide. The walls are sixteen feet in height.

On the west, at regular intervals, six side corridors open off the main corridor. These side corridors open at the other end, westward to the sea. They are much smaller than the main corridor. A seventh corridor which has no opening to the sea is curved. Then, as you move down the main corridor from the entrance, half way along on your left, you find the entrances to three small rooms housing baths. These rectangular rooms are side by side.

At the end of the main corridor are three larger rooms. The one into which the corridor opens is 24 feet square. This is where the Sybil told fortunes. To the west is another room of the same dimensions and this was probably where the consultants stood to hear their fortunes told. The third room, to the east of the first, is larger than the other two. It is thirty feet square. There are two smaller rooms, one to the north and one to the south, opening from this last room.

Text (s)

Very early houses were made of wood and had stones piled around the base to stop the walls from sliding outwards. Their roofs were turfed. In building these houses the first step was to dig a rectangular hole in the ground to allow for enough headroom. Next, stone supports were constructed by piling stones along each side of the hole. Next a forked pole was fixed at each end of the hole to support a ridge pole which was laid across them. Rafters were leaned along each side of the house. These rafters were poles that had been cut all to the same length. Finally, to make the roof, the branches were laid

across the rafters and covered with squares of turf that had been cut from adjoining grassland.
➔ *Now turn to the KEY.*

4.3   Implications for Syllabus Design

It has been implicit with regard to the tasks and discussion of transition notes above that for successful learning "core" form of language which, according to McEldowney (1984:8ff), represents a level of minimum competence. She argues that from this core we can develop more and more sophisticated levels of expressing information. For instance, Texts 4, 8 & 12 used in the case study reported in Chapter Three represent a relatively sophisticated version of instructions, narrative and stative description. Texts 4a, 8a and 12a below illustrate what can be considered grammatically "core" versions of the basic information involved.

> **Text 4a** *(Core Instructions)*
> *Mix the ingredients. Cut up the butter. Knead the mixture. Tip out the mixture. Flatten it. Cut out some biscuits. Bake the biscuits.*

Each of the sentences here is of the VO type and, according to McEldowney's definition of core (ibid), each sentence element contains only one piece of information. As a result, the number of vocabulary items to be dealt with is limited. The six basic steps of the original are expressed in the core version illustrated but all additional information has been stripped from the skeleton.

Adverbial information could be added to each sentence above to produce sentences of the VOA type so extending the range of lexis involved. If each adverbial similarly contains only one piece of information we would still have a core version though there is an additional sentence component to increase the degree of complexity even at this level:

Text 4a(i)
Mix the ingredients in a bowl. Cut up the butter with a knife. Knead the mixture with your fingers. Tip out the mixture in front of you. Flatten it to 1 cm thick. Make biscuits with a cutter. Put them on a tray. Bake the biscuits for 20 minutes. Take the tray out of the oven. Place it on a board.

We note the relatively more sophisticated sentence structure represented by *Use the knife to cut up the butter* has been reduced to *Cut up the butter with a knife.*

The advice in the source text expressed by *You may need to put flour on the work surface to keep the mixture from sticking* and *make sure that their edges do not touch* represent a level of sophistication greater than the versions just illustrated. They are much more grammatically complex and provide an example of two types of instruction being combined together. In the early stages of production learners might be encouraged to produce parallel forms like *make sure their edges do not touch* and *make sure the mixture does not stick.*

A further element of sophistication in the source text is represented by the descriptive elements embedded into adverbial clauses *(Knead the mixture)* until the flour and the sugar are blended into the butter and the mixture is sticky and *(Place the tray on a wooden board)* so that the tray does not burn the work surface. These forms provide more advice of the type referred to in the previous paragraph. They might be expressed in the form *Make sure the flour and sugar blends into the butter* and *Make sure the tray does not burn the work surface*. At the level at which they might be added to the learner's output we might then find:

Text 4a(ii)
Mix the ingredients in a bowl. Cut up the butter with a knife. Knead the mixture with your fingers. <u>Make sure the flour and sugar blends with the butter and make sure the mixture is sticky</u>. Tip out the mixture in front of you. Flatten it to 1 cm thick. <u>Make sure the mixture does not stick.</u> Make biscuits with a cutter. Put them on a tray. <u>Make sure the edges do not touch.</u> Bake the biscuits for 20 minutes. Take the tray out of the oven. Place it on a board. <u>Make sure the work surface does not burn</u>.

In the same way with regard to narrative, Text 8a shows a core version of the narrative sequence of the source text. Each sentence element has only one piece of information:

Text 8a
Some Chinese arrived at dawn. The bishop went with them. He tended the wounded.

As we saw in the case of instructions, we can add greater complexity even at the core level by including additional sentence components, each of which contains only one piece of information:

Text 8a(ii)
The Chinese arrived at the mission at dawn. The bishop went with them to the hospital. He tended the wounded with his medicines.

More information is carried in descriptive comments in the original providing a higher level of textual complexity. At a higher level this can be added to the core sequence thus:

Text 8a(iii)
The Chinese arrived at the mission at dawn. They were armed. The bishop had some medicines. The Chinese wanted his help. The bishop trusted them. He went with them to the hospital. He tended the wounded. There were 13 or 14.

We note that this descriptive information provides the reasons for the events in the basic narrative sequence.

If we turn to the information about guinea pigs in Text 12 we note that a simpler version of the stative description might read something like:

Text 12a
Pets
Guinea pigs are called cavies. Some are smooth-haired. These are hardy. They eat little. They eat greens, carrots, turnips, apple peel and bread. In summer they crop grass. In winter they like bran each night. They need water. They live up to 8 years.

Of significance here is the way in which the more complex noun phrase of the original is broken down. The noun phrase the *more hardy smooth-haired kind* contains more than one idea. In the core version each idea has its own sentence. – *Some are smooth-haired. These are hardy.* This phenomenon of complex noun phrases which embed several ideas is a feature of all communicative purposes. For instance, in the narrative text we find the phrase *a strange deputation* describing the Chinese. If this were to be simplified learners might be expected to produce. *A deputation arrived at the mission. They were strange.....*

We note that, if the information about their living and protection is reduced to core form, it is basically instructional. For instance, an adjectival form like *raised*, in *Cavies like raised cages*, essentially embeds a core instruction into a descriptive context – Raise their cages (McEldowney, ibid). Thus, added to the description about a suitable type of guinea pig for keeping as a pet, their food and life span, we might add instructions for their care:

Text 8a(i)
Guinea pigs are called cavies[5]. Some are smooth-haired. These are hardy. <u>Choose this type for pets. Raise their cages. Put in some hay for their beds.</u> They eat little. They eat greens, carrots, turnips, apple peel and bread. In summer they crop grass. <u>Enclose them in the garden.</u>

---

[5] Notice that the form *are called* can be considered as a core phrase to be learned by heart in such a context. *Guinea pigs are cavies* does not seem to be an appropriate form of expression. A similar form is seen n the case of *was born* in something like *Shakespeare was born in Stratford* (Compare *Shakespeare's mother bore him in Stratford*).

Protect them. In winter they like bran each night. Heat it. They need much water. Put it in a bottle. Change it each day. They live up to 8 years.

As we shall see below in our discussion of an appropriate methodology, core versions like those illustrated above can be produced by our learners from tasks related to original source texts. We have seen above how complexity can develop even at the core level by, for instance, adding further sentence components and by putting two communicative purposes together. As we move on further in a systematic manner, the level of complexity required from our learners will depend on their ability and stage of learning in an overall move from core to more and more sophisticated ways of communicating textual information.

We note, further, that the example of description represented by the information about guinea pigs is a generalisation. Such description should be preceded by specific description in learning terms. For instance, information about individual examples of items like a range of different pencils, different cars, different houses must precede a generalisation about pencils, cars or houses, that integrates the common features of the class. So, for instance, there is a one-to-one match between words and example in the real world in something like *This pencil is red. It is wooden. It contains lead. It is 2 inches long* or *This pencil is green. It is plastic. It contains lead. It is 4 inches long. and so on.* It is only after the conceptual and linguistic achievement of such expression that the learner can move on to the generalisation which is an abstraction of all the pencils in the world and which will be grammatically more sophisticated – Pencils are made of different materials. They may be wooden, plastic, silver or gold. They are of different colours. Some are of a fixed length while others are made of wood that can be sharpened and so reduced in length. They all contain lead for......

Thus, it would seem that textual material should develop on the basis of several dichotomies:

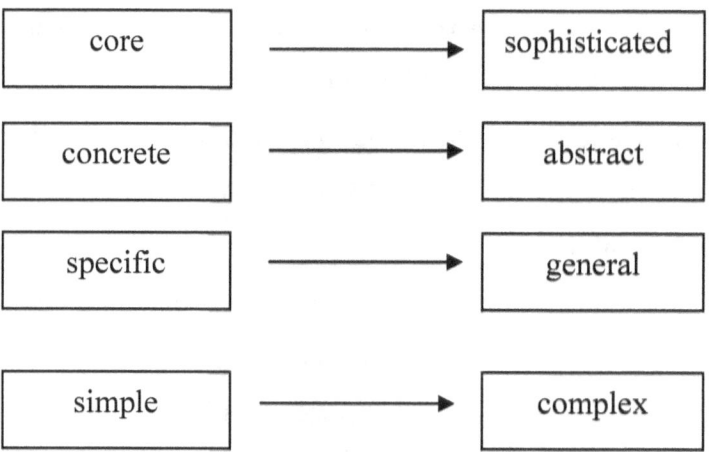

This suggests the following development with regard to communicative purpose:

specific instruction
specific description
general instruction
general description
narration

At suitable stages in this development two purposes might be mixed. So, for instance, once a learner is in control of specific instructions and specific description, the two might be combined. Thus, a sequence of instructions for making a specific item might be followed by a paragraph describing the finished product.

4.4   Classroom Use

In their preparation, once teachers have developed transition notes, they need to develop appropriate tasks for classroom use. For instance, with regard to the instructions, the teacher needs to lead the class to identify the sequence of imperative verbs as the central carrier of meaning in the source text. In the early stages of learning the teacher might provide the verbs in jumbled order and then ask the learners to read (or listen to) the text and number the steps in the order they need to be carried out. Once learners have some experience they might be asked merely to identify the steps and list the verbs involved. Once learners have identified the appropriate steps, they can provide the teacher with the necessary information to list the steps on the chalkboard, whiteboard or OHP. The same process is carried out with the "whats", the "wheres" the "instruments" and so on until the transition notes have been completed and written where the whole class can see them. Thus, without worrying too much about meaning, learners have been encouraged to identify in a systematic way the linguistic categories appropriate to developing instructive sentences. At this stage McEldowney (1996/7a:5) suggests that language learners might, following the model provided by the teacher, use the notes to practise the music of the language by orally reconstructing the sentences. The reconstructed instructions will be simpler in form that the source text in the way indicated above in 4.4. This activity will also provide preparation for later writing up of the instructions.

After such tasks which help build up linguistic awareness and prosodic skill, the teacher will need to turn to meaning. This might involve, initially, some speculation about the meaning of any words that are perhaps unfamiliar but, before recourse to dictionaries, learners might be presented with a set of visuals in which the steps are in random order. They would then be asked to label some sugar, some flour, some butter, ingredients, the mixture, a bowl, the work surface and the like. At this point, unfamiliar words may be speculated upon in a trial and error manner.

After work with the ingredients and apparatus to be used in the recipe, attention should turn to the sequence of steps. In this case the teacher might ask the learners to find a suitable imperative verb for each diagram in the sequence. Finally, the learners will be asked to put the diagrams in the correct order for carrying out the instructions.

Once this has been achieved, the labelled diagrams can be used for the learners to outline the steps orally and then to write up the instructions they have thus rehearsed. At this point mono-lingual dictionaries might be used to confirm any meanings that learners still feel insecure about.

A similar process will be carried out with regard to narrative. Learners will build up transition notes by identifying the sequence of past tense verbs, the sentence subjects, objects and adverbials. Then, after a spoken rehearsal, they might label and order a series of narrative pictures presented out of order. These will then be the basis for further spoken rehearsal for the writing of the story.

With regard to stative description, learners might be presented with a table to fill in. This table will then be the basis for spoken practice. Here a teacher might want to alert learners to the use of a particular structure within the context. For instance, in the example above we suggested that the use of an asterisk might remind learners to use a construction with should. Such practice might be followed by work on identifying, from appropriate drawings, a smooth-haired guinea pig, an appropriate raised cage filled with hay and the like. The table then provides the stimulus for written production. [6]

In this way, learners develop the skills of comprehension and production around a specified piece of information. Rather

---

[6] The appendix details two pieces of learning material developed by McEldowney, one for a sequenced text and one for stative description

than discussing the meaning of unfamiliar words at the beginning of the session, meaning is allowed to develop as activities progress. This means that learners are more likely to develop the skill of inferring meaning from context and thus a better overall textual awareness. They will not feel insecure when they come across unfamiliar items and feel over-faced with the task. The process can be seen to be one of analysing and synthesising in a move to discover the maximum meaning appropriate to the level of learning involved. A source text is analysed to produce transition notes and a final

synthesis results in the production of a piece of cohesive text. The process can be summarised thus

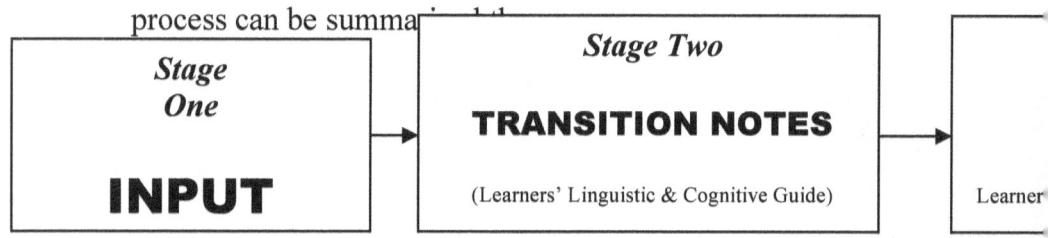

Stage One

INPUT

Stage Two

TRANSITION NOTES

(Learners' Linguistic & Cognitive Guide)

Learner

LEARNING TASKS

For language learners the information cycle stops at this point and learning proceeds with exposure to more and more input texts at increasing levels of difficulty and with less and less teacher control, the aim being to equip the learner to manipulate information as independently as possible. In learning to translate, however, a further dimension needs to be added to the information cycle outlined above.

4.5   Translation

In learning to translate, Stage Two B and Stage Three B need to be added:

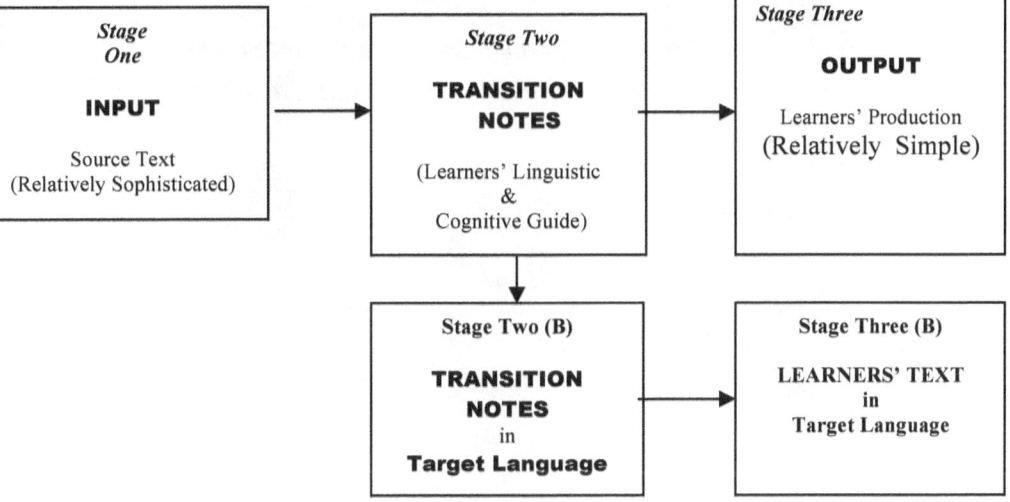

Thus, learners recycle the information from the source text (in this case English) in order to improve their comprehension and productive skills in this additional language and to create an awareness of the central features of the source text. They then develop transition notes in the target language (in this case Arabic) which show the organisation and grammatical markers appropriate to expressing the information of the source text in the target language. After oral rehearsal this is then used to produce a text in the source language. This process, it is argued, will lead to an accurate translation with minimum information loss or the inclusion of excess information.

The use of transition notes in the way suggested is more likely to control the tendency of learners to try for a word-for-word translation. The shift from one language to another in the way described throws the emphasis on context rather than individual vocabulary items. Further, as they are working from notes rather than text, learners are more likely to produce an Arabic text which is coherent in Arabic as they inflate the notes to formulate text.

Modelled on the English transition notes illustrated above in 7.4.2, appropriate transition notes in Arabic for each of Text 4, 8 and 12 might be as follows.

Text 4

اخلط   المقادير   في الإناء

قطع   الزبد

اخلط   الدقيق والسكر   مع الزبد   بأصابعك

ضع   بعض الدقيق

اكفت   الخليط

افرد   الخليط

اصنع   بعض البسكويت

ضع   البسكويت   في صينية الخبز

شغل   الفرن   على علامة 4

اخبز   البسكويت   لمدة 20 دقيقة

اخرج   البسكويت   من الفرن   (مستخدما) قطعة قماش

ضع   الصينية   على طاولة العمل

Text 8

وصل   بعض الصينيين   إلى البعثة

مسلحين

طلب   الصينيون   من المطران

الذهاب معهم   أدوية

ذهب   المطران   معهم

للمستشفى

إعتنى   المطران   بالجرحى   ثلاثة عشر

جريحا

Text 12

	خنزير غينيا
الكابياء	الاسم الصحيح
حيوانات أليفة	الهدف
الشعر الناعم-القوية	النوع المناسب
عالية	الأقفاص
الأوراق الخضراء،الجزر اللفت ، قشور التفاح، الخبز، الخلطة الخاصة	الطعام الأساسي
العشب	طعام الصيف
النخالة	طعام الشتاء
الكثير من الماء العذب	الماء
ثمان سنوات	العمر المتوقع

As we can see from the Arabic transition notes above, it is possible to control the linguistic system of both languages to ensure maximum coherence. The similarities and differences between the two systems can be made clear. In the case of the major textual features of instruction and narrative we can see there is little difference between the two language systems. With regard to pronominal usage, however, as we saw in our discussion of textual coherence in Chapter Three, there are slight differences of emphasis. We saw above how the English notes control determiner usage and pronominal reference according to the English norm. In Arabic, however, the it in the "what" column after flatten becomes the mixture الخلط and, similarly, the them following lay becomes the biscuits البسكويت, a phenomenon typical of Arabic. Such points should be discussed with learners as they prepare their Arabic transition notes and before spoken and written production in Arabic.

4.6   Conclusion

In the early stages of learning a language and in the early stages of learning to translate it, the aim is to minimise the amount of negotiation involved in order to ensure maximum accuracy. To carry out this aim, work can most effectively begin with transactional text which, in addition, has a central role in education. An information cycle which enables learners to gather textual information through the exercise of their listening and reading skills and to reproduce it in spoken and written mode, first in the source language and then in the target language, can be controlled through the development of transition notes. The notes provide a "map" of appropriate linguistic form and textual meaning for the learner. The goal is for learners to develop independence in the use of this cycle as quickly as possible.

Learners need to go on to develop skill with more and more complex transactional language and, at an appropriate time, begin to develop their interactive skills beyond those involved in working together on the tasks involved in the basic information cycle. Further, each individual has a set of *complex intentions with regard to communication and needs to be able to express these in a manner acceptable to whatever situation is involved. This quite quickly involves a move beyond the "norm" represented by transactional language. Individuals need to become dextrous recipients and producers of language beyond the norm if they are to survive in the "real" world and communicate in an acceptable way in whatever situation they find themselves. The final achievement is an interpreter who can work effectively in very controversial situations or a translator who can produce a poem that is as great a piece of art in a target language as it was in the source language.*

Chapter Five

Language Beyond the Norm

5.1 Introduction

In communicating, the producer of a piece of language constructs a closely-knit pattern of grammatical dependencies and syntax to convey information. The receiver of the language processes the mismatch *between the configuration of concepts* and *prior knowledge of the world* (Beaugrande & Dressler, 1981:84). As we have seen in transactional language the system is relatively controllable and the balance between intention and acceptability is easily maintained but the network of options available to the language user goes far beyond this norm.

Our discussion of transactional language concentrated on the mode of delivery of pieces of language and thus basically covered only the illocutionary act, that is, *encoding a set of notions into lexical items arranged according to the constraints of English syntax* (Hatim & Mason, 1997:60). A consideration of other types of language, however, indicates that the effect of utterances on the receiver may vary to a much greater degree. In this case, we need to look at the perlocutionary act, the effect of the producer's intentions, (planned or unplanned) on the receiver.

A speaker or writer uses utterances to relay messages. In an utterance like *Can you pass the ketchup?,* the speaker is apparently asking about the hearer's ability to pass the ketchup. The actual meaning, however, is a request to pass the ketchup. There is a pragmatic intention *bearing on the illocutionary force of the utterance* (Recanati, 1987:25). In this respect, Austin (1962) refers to the ability of sentences to perform actions. He says that performatives, in contrast to statements, have dynamic communicative purposes and can move communication forward, explaining the ways in which these performatives can go wrong or can be "unhappy" or "infelicitous". Further, the perlocutionary effect intended by the producer of a piece of language may be different to the actual effect on the receiver as the producer cannot always have control of the receiver's reactions. For instance, an utterance like *I am hungry* may have been meant merely as a statement of fact but the hearer may, however, have produced a banana or a piece of cake in reply, something not intended by the speaker.

The purpose of what follows is to indicate, in more detail than in Chapter One, the complex network of options available to language users in the communication of information and to show how various ambiguities must be resolved in the attempt to ensure acceptability as information is conveyed.

5.2   The Complexities of Spoken Language

Spoken language is the embodiment of social language which by its very nature goes beyond the norms of transactional language. It is personal and unpredictable. Hence, acceptability is not always straightforward and conveyance of information may be complex. To examine this situation, let us consider Text 21 below and then examine the complexities that arise when the same information is related in the spoken mode.

Text 21

One evening, Dr Oh was resting after a particularly hard day in the plague-infested village when there was a small knock on the door. "Come in!" he called. A small wizened woman entered timidly. She was probably under forty, but she appeared much older. "It's my daughter, doctor. She's very ill." the woman said in a hoarse voice. "I'll tell you what I will do," he said. "I'll give you some medicine for your daughter to take tonight".

"No, doctor. Please. She is my only daughter and she is terribly sick," she said. Dr Oh could see that she could not be dissuaded and he picked up his umbrella and followed her in the dark through the rain. Soon after they reached the village outside the town Dr Oh suddenly realised there were no more footsteps in front of him. When he looked up he could see in front of him an ordinary village home. The woman was no longer in sight. Dr Oh reached into his bag and brought out an electric torch. He pushed aside the half-open front door and walked into the house. There was no one in the main room. Then he entered the bedroom and his light revealed the forms of a woman and a girl lying in the corner.

Dr Oh went to the figures and examined them. The girl was a plague victim and had been dead for an hour. He

then turned to the woman. He could hardly believe his
eyes. She was certainly the same woman who had led him
to the house minutes before, but by every indication she
had been dead at least four days. And that is exactly how
Dr Oh recorded it later in his diary, as a testimony to a
mother's love. (Ong, et al 1977:91-92)

The series of events narrated here is relatively straightforward
and the role of the characters involved quite clear.

Hatim & Mason (1997:15) consider a text to be cohesive when
the various components of the surface text (the actual words we
see) are mutually connected within a sequence of some kind. As
is typical of narrative (2.2.2) a central coherence is created by the
sequence of stem+*ed* forms (*picked up, followed, reached,*
realised, looked up and so on) which carry forward the events and
provide the essential framework for what is being related. This
framework is filled out by the switch, at appropriate places, to
descriptive comment which provides information, for instance,
about the appearance of the woman and the scene within the
house. The direct speech integrated into appropriate parts of the
narrative helps to bring the scene to life as the characters interact
with each other. The development of the relationship between the
characters and the moment of illumination or denouement enables
the reader to experience what happened through the mind of the
main character.

At a more detailed level, grammatical cohesion is also maintained, for instance, by anaphoric reference. In Text 21, pronominal usage has this anaphoric function as in the use of *he* and *she* to refer back to the respective characters Dr Oh, the woman and the girl. Similarly, there is anaphoric reference with regard to determiner usage as, for instance, in *the half-open door*, *the house, the main room, the bedroom* where *the* marks reference back to *an ordinary village home* where "first mention" is marked by *an*.

As well as grammatical cohesion, Hatim & Mason (ibid) point out that the choice of lexis achieves harmony in text. Lexical cohesion is maintained in Text 21 through the reiteration of the same term, the use of synonyms and the use of collocation (*medicine-take-tonight; umbrella-dark-rain; doctor-examined; plague-victim-dead; recorded-diary*).

We use the same language when we write or speak but *the size and shapes of sentences tend to be different* (Bygate, 1987:14). Pop music, jazz and orchestral music use the same notes and scales but they differ in the way these notes and scales are blended. The same can be said about spoken and written language *and the reason for this is largely to do with the constraints under which language is produced* (ibid). These constraints may be referred to as "processing conditions" and the question arises as to the significance of these features for the translator. As we shall see later, there are situations when it might be necessary to include features of the processing conditions and others when they are extremely significant. Whatever the case, it is clear that the translator should be aware of the nature of the complexities of speech in both the source and target languages.

To illustrate how speech differs from written text, a small experiment required a native speaker teacher of English to pass the information in Text 21 on to her twenty-year old non-native English speaking students by means of a spoken monologue. The result is transcribed in Text 22 below. Another native speaker of English was asked to tell the story to her four young daughters. This version is transcribed in Text 23.

Text 22

There was this doctor who was working in a plague-infested area. He worked in a town and one day there .... someone came knocking at his door. And he opened the door and there was this wizened old woman saying "Oh please! Please! Come to my house very quickly. She ....she's very sick". "Oh", said the doctor. Well, it was quite late. "I'll give you some medicine and you give her ... I'm sure that'll be OK.". "Please, she's my only daughter. You must come NOW". She was begging him and in the end he gave in.

So. He followed her off. It was night time.... He followed her off into the night. And (cough). They were walking in the dark. Suddenly, he was aware <u>that there were no other footsteps except his own!</u> He couldn't hear the woman's footsteps – <u>she was walking by his side.</u> And she disappeared. So. He took out a torch. <u>He often needed to find his way in the dark when he was visiting sick people in the surrounding villages. He took out his torch</u> and there was no sign of the woman. <u>No sign of her anywhere. So what else could he do?</u> He carried on...<u>He knew where her house was in the village and it wasn't far to go. He carried on walking till he came to the village</u> and saw the house and the front door was open. So he knocked but there was *no reply. No answer at all. So he walked in and there was no one there. There was the ... the sitting room was empty so he walked around calling her name quietly till ...then he came to the bedroom and there were two bodies laying in the corner of the room and he went up to them and one of them was a young girl who had obviously been dead for about four days. And* [long pause] *no. there was a girl who'd just died maybe about an hour before ...her body was still warmish. And next to her was the woman, the one who came to his house who had walked down the road with him. Presumably the mother...who'd been dead for four days. He could tell cos of course he was a doctor and knew these things. The doctor was amazed and he wrote down later to remember and tell people He just was moved that the mother loved her daughter that she came back from the dead to try and get the doctor to save her life. She'd obviously come back because she knew she was dying. I think that's amazing, don't you?*

Text 23

Listen girls. This is a ghost story....Not all ghost stories are frightening. Some are lovely tales – yeah, lovely tales. You know they tell us about... of kindness and love. Once there was a hard-working man called Dr Oh who lived during a time of plague. You don't know what a plague is. Well...this is when there is a bad sickness that affects many people. One night Dr Oh was resting after a hard day. There was a knock at his door, and a small tired-looking woman spoke to him. "Please come and tend to my daughter, to my daughter". Dr Oh was very tired and said to her, "I'll visit her tomorrow. Take this medicine for her, just for tonight." "No, no that will never do! Please, she is my only daughter and she is very sick. You must come with me now!" exclaimed the woman. So, seeing that he could not change her mind and because he had a kind heart, Dr Oh agreed to see her daughter. He followed her through the dark rainy night. They reached a village. Dr Oh could not hear the woman's footsteps. He looked around for the woman but all that he saw was a small house. Confused, Dr Oh stepped through the open door of the house. At first, he saw no one, but then he noticed two figures lying in the corner of the room. It was hard for him to see as it was dark and gloomy. He went to the first figure and saw that it was a young girl. He realised that she had been dead for about an hour – another victim of the plague – turned to the other person. He couldn't believe his eyes! It was the same person that had come to his home and had led him to this house. But he soon realised that she was also dead – but dead for at least four days! How could that be? Yes...I'll tell you. Dr Oh believes the.. that the mother loved her daughter so much that even after death she wanted to help her daughter. What do you think?

5.2.1 Adapting to an Audience

One essential difference between the three versions of the story given in the previous section is related to the audience involved. In the case of the original written version in Text 21 we note that the audience is unknown to the writer. A mutual understanding of the world is assumed. In the case of the two spoken versions of the information, however, the audience was present while the story was being told. Speakers tend to alter their delivery to suit the age, level of education, linguistic competence, experience and the like of their audience. The teacher speaking to her class of 20 year old non-native speakers (Text 22) was keen to avoid any obscurity or ambiguity and so left little for her learners to interpret or fill in for themselves. The extra information she felt necessary is underlined in the text. The teacher's aim was educational. She wanted her class to understand as clearly as possible. The result is a version much less dense and concise than the written version. At one level her spoken version appears to be less coherent than the written version but the cohesion is of a different type. It is related to her need to educate her audience.

Text 23 indicates a different purpose on the part of the mother talking to her daughters. She is telling a story and resorts to the "once upon a time" story convention in *Once there was a hard-working man called Dr Oh.* She is very aware of her audience and ensures that she imparts the information at a level that they will understand. The dense *Dr Oh was resting after a particularly hard day in the plague-infested village when there was a small knock on the door* of the written version is, for instance, broken down, simplified and clarified – *Once there was a hard-working man called Dr Oh who lived during a time of plague* [explanation of what plague is]. *One night* [implicit but not mentioned in the written version] *Dr Oh was resting after a hard day...* Because her audience are young the mother begins by reassuring them about the nature of ghost stories. Perhaps also because of the youth of her audience and her relationship with them she chooses to say that the plague "affects" people rather than "kills" them.

In the written original of Text 21 the moment of illumination i.e. the final unravelling of the story when the plot is resolved, *She was certainly the same woman who led him to the house minutes before, but by every indication she had been dead for at least four days*, leaves readers to come to their own conclusion. For artistic reasons the writer does not state the obvious (though then he spoils the moment by adding the didactic comment *and that is exactly how Dr Oh recorded it in his diary, as a testimony to a mother's love.*) Both speakers, however, feel the need to explain the situation rather than leaving it to their listeners' imagination. Both also end by a direct appeal to their audience – *I think that's amazing, don't you* (Text 22) and *What do you think?* (Text 23).

In the written version of the story represented by Text 21 the information stands in its own right without the intervention of "unnecessary" explanation. There is apparently a greater coherence. Further, the flow of speech may be deflected by audience participation in a way that cannot happen with regard to written communication. Not only must the information be conveyed in a way suitable to what the speaker perceives to be the needs of the audience but also speakers must often modify their original plan as a result of feedback from the audience. For instance, the mother's explanation of what plague was in Text 23 is cued by a question from one of her daughters. We note that, in a different situation, the audience might not be satisfied with the general statement that the plague "affects" people and might negotiate further explanation perhaps by asking in what way it has an affect. This audience, however, seem to trust its mother's wisdom and is also anxious to discover what comes next.

It is interesting to note in this respect that the mother could not avoid an interruption at the moment of illumination. To prevent it spoiling the continuity of the story, however, she repeats the question of one of her daughters (*How could that be?*) and integrates it within the narrative. The repetition of the interlocutor's words gives the speaker time to put her thoughts in order and the question is followed by a straightforward analysis of the situation. She is aware that her audience is concerned with the "how", "what" and "why" which are the source of artistic enjoyment.

Successful spoken communication requires the special ability of the speaker to react appropriately to the listener.

Humans are endowed with the potential to allow them to predict, adapt and act in response to others. As we have just seen they, may need to respond to verbal stimuli. Alternatively, eye contact will signal to what extent an audience is accepting the message. In Text 23, there was perhaps no such clue as to how the children felt, prompting the mother to ask *What do you think?*

5.2.2 False Starts, Hesitation, Repetition, Rephrasing

Unlike written language, which can be reworked until the writer is satisfied, spoken language shows the marks of its more ephemeral nature. A speaker is thinking and planning in a much more ad hoc manner than a writer. As a result the speaker may start, abort and restart again. We have already seen how the story-teller of Text 23 begins by reassuring her daughters about the nature of ghost stories. This was perhaps not part of her original plan. Ad hoc behaviour is suggested by a short hesitation, the repetition of *lovely tales,* the *yeah* and the *you know.* After she has responded to a question about the plague the story flows relatively smoothly.

The type of repetition just referred to is another feature typical of spoken language. Ideas may be repeated by using the same words, as in the example above, or speakers may use a different expression either for emphasis or to give themselves time to think. In Text 22 we find *He followed her off. It was night time ... He followed her off into the night.* This seems to provide an example of rephrasing and a false start as the speaker organises her thoughts. As they talk speakers make slight changes to the structure bearing the message in order *to ram home the point in the listener's brain while giving themselves time to mentally prepare for the next point* (Burgess: 1990:9).

Speech is also marked by the use of fillers and hesitation devices as a strategy to give speakers time to organise their ideas. The two speakers of Text 22 and 23 are relatively practiced in the sort of delivery illustrated. Also, each had time to think about the information before producing her spoken version. As a result there is relatively little hesitation in contrast to the following from Bygate (1987:18):

> *OK – erm-a at the back (mhm) I mean we – in the office I also see a – this is a young lady (Mhm) sitting in a chair (Mhm) she might be a secretary (mhm) – OK – it seems to me Oh th this er little boy (mhm) this little boy seems to be – punished don't you see – he has er – he has his hands – in the back*

where we see a great deal of hesitation and many false starts to the extent that the flow of information is quite severely disrupted.

5.2.3 Simplifying Structure

Simplifying structure is, according to Bygate (1987:15), another feature of the immediacy of speech. He says that it is easier for speakers to improvise when they use simple structures. We have already referred to this phenomenon in 5.2.1 with regard to the beginning of the mother's story in Text 23. In this case an awareness of the youth of her listeners worked together with the normal tendency towards simplification of structure in the spoken mode.

With regard to simplification, Bygate (ibid) further points out that speakers tend to link new sentences with previous ones by using co-ordinating conjunctions like *and* and *but* or no conjunction at all. Such parataxis is a feature of Text 22. He says also that speakers avoid the use of adjectives preceding the noun to form complex noun groups and tend to add adjectives separately – *He saw a dog, big and brown.* Ellipsis, which involves omitting part of a sentence, enables speakers to produce information in a more economical way as we saw in 1.7 in the text where the speakers discussed the weather – *not bad really. Could be worse.* We do not always relay oral messages in complete sentences.

5.2.4 Formulaic Expressions

Spoken language makes use of colloquial or idiomatic expressions in a way not considered appropriate to written language:

1   *(in a bar) Have this one on me.*
2.   *I thought you'd never ask*
3.   *What does he think he is?*
(cited in Stubbs, 1983:155)

Such expressions represent an awareness of meaning far beyond the transactional, relying on a high level of cultural experience, and require a great deal of negotiation on the part of the translator.

5.3 Acceptability

To allow for ease of communication a piece of language must be acceptable to the reader or listener. A degree of complexity is presented to the translator where there is lack of cohesion, irrelevant situationality, inadequate informativity and a failure to perceive intertextuality. To control these features skilled language users employ the external aspect of language. Bell (1991: 172) explains the internal aspect of language as being what it **is** as a context-free code and indicates that the external aspect is what language is **for** – i.e. *the functions of language as a context-sensitive communication system.*

5.3.1 Cohesion & Coherence

As we have seen, in a stream of speech chunks of information are managed by speaker and listener as the former produces them to relay a message and the latter is involved in interpreting it. In writing, because normally writers do not act under constraint, it is possible for them to have second thoughts and to rewrite sections. If written texts do not adhere to "normal" features of cohesion and coherence, communication may break down as there is no possibility of direct negotiation with the reader. For instance, in the following extract from Rushdie's *Satanic Verses* we see a coherence which is hard to grasp. Normally, meaning depends on knowledge gleaned from adjacent sentences. Here, however, the meaning is dependent on an intricate linkage ambiguously woven into the story. Elements within the extract are not dependent for their meaning on surrounding context. Readers rely for meaning on

- information dispersed throughout the story

- assumption

- pre-knowledge not articulated on the surface.

Text 24

The businessman: Looks as he should, high forehead, eaglenose, broad in the shoulders, narrow in the hip. Average height, brooding, dressed in two pieces of plain cloth, each four ells in length, one draped around his body, the other over his shoulder. Large eyes; long lashes like a girl's. His strides can seem too long for his legs, but he's a light-footed man. Orphans learn to be moving targets, develop a rapid walk, quick reactions, hold-your-tongue caution. Up through the thorn bushes and opobalsm trees he comes, scrabbling on boulders, this is a fit man, no soft-bellied usurer he. And yes, to state it again: takes an odd sort of business wallah to cut off into the wilds, up Mount Cone, sometimes for a month at a stretch, just to be alone.

His name: a dream-name, changed by the vision. Pronounced correctly, it means he-for-whom-thanks-should-be-given, but he won't answer to that here; nor, though he's well aware of what they call him, his nickname in Jahilia down below - "he-who-goes-up-and-down-old-Coney". Here he is neither Mahomet nor MoeHammered; has adopted, instead, the demon-tag the

farangis hung around his neck. To turn insults into
strengths, whigs, tories, Blacks all chose to wear with
pride the names they were given in scorn; likewise, our
mountain-climbing, prophet-motivated solitary is to be the
medieval baby-frightener, the Devil's synonym: Mahound.
That's him. Mahound the businessman, climbing
his hot mountain in the Hijaz. The mirage of a city shines
below him in the sun.(Rushdie, 1988:93)

Rushdie unravels the complications of the situation depicted here by using complex and ambiguous cohesive elements. The text does not rely on normal sentence links but on a complex web of implicit connections in meaning. In his effort to depict the image of the Prophet Mohamed he refers to a businessman, describing what he should be like. He then refers to the fact (of which Moslems are aware) that he is an "orphan", "a light-footed man" and goes on to comment on the nature of orphans – "orphans are like that"...

In this description the writer relies very little on conventional reference words, believing that his readers will eventually realise about whom he is speaking. He employs a strategy of delaying clarification. There are sentences which leave the reader hanging – *orphans learn to be moving targets* or *His name, a dream name*. Then he unravels the ideas gradually until he cries out *That's him: Mahound*. In the middle of the description he translates the Prophet's name into English – *he-for-whom-thanks-should-be-given* and concludes with *That's him. Mahound the businessman,* a distortion of Mohamed's name which associates it with a hound. The writer makes a great effort to squeeze out a personal hatred, delaying clarification as chunk after chunk provides only part of an answer.

5.3.2 Textuality

Another aspect of failure to communicate is when text is not relevant to the situation in which it occurs. An eavesdropper not involved in the interaction or unaware of the culture in which it is produced might find it difficult to follow the drift in

> *I am sorry if er ... shall we go and have a bite to ...? Or have you had your ..... Oh, by the way, we can't , go in my ... you see, I've failed my ... Ugh, the examiner was an absolute ...*
> (cited in Stubbs, 1983:155)

It becomes acceptable, however, when placed in context – two friends meeting at Oxford Circus, just before lunch after one has just failed his driving test.

An Arabic text from a short story by the Jordanian writer Ibrahim Za'rour illustrates how a failure to relate text to situation might cause a misinterpretation of the writer's intention and thus lead to unacceptability.

Text 25

ففي إحدى نزوات ما بعد الظهيرة- التي عرف بها رحمه الله ايام القيظ – تباهى، وبتحريض جلساء الوالي التركي، وتبرع بقطعة الأرض الممتدة ما بين المسجد وساحة الجلود، وأوقفها – لوجه الله تعالى – على المطلقات من جواري الوالي ... وجاء في الصفحة الثانية والخمسين من كتاب "الأعاجيب في نكت الرعابيب" الذي عثرت عليه في رحلتي اللاحقة، إن خير

الدين بن زرد فدمات بعد ظهيرة اليوم التالي كمدا بعد ان بلغ مسامعه ما تندرت به جواري الوالي بما كان من طيشه وخفة عقله.. حيث مات بعد أن كان فرغ لتوه من تعليق شملته على الوتد المخصص لها على جدار بيته الرطب وبدأ يتخفف من زناره ذي الأربع عشرة طية عندما تهاوى جثة هامدة تاركا اثنتين من حريمه حوامل في شهورهما الأخيرة

(زعرور - مكان

ضيق شديد الضيق 1997 ص 11)

Text 25

[In one of the afternoon whimsical acts which, Allah bless his soul, was known for, he showed off and with provocation from the Turkish Governor's (Wali's) companions offered the piece of land stretching from the mosque to the leather area and trusted it – for the sake of Allah's Face – to the divorced maids (Jawari) of the Governor. On page 52 of *Kitab al-a'ajeeb fi nukaat al-ra'abeeb* which I came across later on in my journey, Khair Ed Din Bin Zard died of grief on the afternoon of the next day when he heard how the maids made fun of his light-headedness and rashness. He died immediately after hanging his cloak on a special peg on the damp wall in his house as he began to slip out of the fourteen-fold girdle. He fell dead, leaving behind two of his harems in their last months of pregnancy.]

(Za'rour, 1997:11) (Translated by Saad, 2002)

Ibrahim Za'rour is a clever storyteller. He can take us smoothly into the world of his tales with the use of very compelling language. He employs the techniques of biography and genuine travel accounts swarming with sarcasm and puns. The extract above gives us the impression that it belongs to a different age placed within the Turkish Empire. This is because of the names of the characters (Khair Eddin Bin Zard and the like); the rhyming nature of the book title, *Kitab al-ajeeb fi nukaat al-ra'abeeb*; the fact that the way of narrating the story is reminiscent of *One Thousand and One Nights*, a method of narration which dominated the writings of the Ottoman Empire; the description of the main character's clothes; the choice of lexis (Wali, harems, Jawari, Turkish and the like); and the number of wives connected with the Wali and Khair Eddin. Then, the description of the lottery dealers as the "marines" or the mention of the "black Mercedes" brings us back to the present time. Once again we jump to a different era and immediately after that we are brought back to the present when the writer describes one of his characters as Marilyn Monroe. Unless the reader is aware of the political and social situation in which the text has its origin, it will be difficult to find the relevance. The writer's aim is to be sarcastic. He is also making sure that he avoids prosecution for mocking a sector of the regime. If such factors are recognised by the reader, the text will achieve the acceptability which depends on its *believability and relevance to the participants' outlook regarding the situation* (Beaugrand & Dressler, 1981:179).

5.3.3 Informativity

When a writer or speaker conveys information it is important that it satisfies the receiver's expectations. It is important to achieve a balance between the amount of information and the length of the text. If the information is too dense for the situation the communication may well not be acceptable to the reader or listener. For instance, if a road sign placed beside the road were something like *Since the road is slippery we would advise the motorists reading this to slow down as soon as possible to prevent them endangering their own lives and those of other road users*, we would not expect passing motorists to read it. They would not have time. More appropriate to the situation is the conventional *Slippery Road* which exploits the redundancy of the language to communicate the sort of information "stuffed into" our previous example (McEldowney, 1993:31).

A defiance of expectation might work well when text is manipulated in such a way as to catch the attention of the reader or listener. In Text 25 above, for instance, Ibrahim Za'rour surprises us with the density of the information about Khair Eddin. He even refers to page 52 of *Kitab al-a'ajeeb fi nukaat al-ra'abeeb* (a book that never existed) to provide accurate and meticulous detail. Present and past are interwoven in a way that might confuse a non-co-operative reader. We experience an explosion of information but the situation is one in which the reader, unlike the motorist referred to above, has time to linger and absorb. Acceptability may, however, be challenged when text requires intricate processing. The artist must maintain a balance and excessive and unexpected words can generate uncertainty, Beaugrande & Dressler (1981:9) suggest that *caution must be exercised lest the receivers' processing become overloaded to the point of endangering communication.*

In Joyce's *Portrait of the Artist as a Young Man*, Father Arnall launches into a lengthy description, blood curdling and horrific in its detail, of the pains of hell which the damned will suffer. Father Arnall repeats the theme. In the morning he speaks of the torments of hell. In the evening he talks about its spiritual torment. He analyses these under the five headings of pain of loss, pain of conscience, pain of extension, pain of intensity and the eternity of pain. It is a long description. Time and time again Joyce, through Father Arnall, draws a horrifying picture:

Text 26
They lie in exterior darkness. For, remember, the fire of hell gives forth no light. As, at the command of God, the fire of the Babylonian *furnace lost its heat but not its light, so, at the command of God, the fire of hell, while retaining the intensity of its heat, burns eternally in darkness. It is a never ending storm of darkness, dark flames and dark smoke of burning brimstone, amid which the bodies are heaped one upon another without even a glimpse of air* (Joyce, 1916:92)

This rather dense description is in danger of hindering communication. A patient reader, however, will even enjoy an element of humour. In Stephen Dedalus' first shock of guilt, shame is redoubled by the thought of Emma (the girl he slept with). Now that God and the Virgin Mary are remote from his filth, it is by picturing Emma at his side that he can rise from his abject inertia. The daydream of himself, hand-in-hand with Emma, being forgiven and comforted by a sympathetic Virgin Mary is a comic piece of self-projection.

It is worth pointing out at this juncture that every text has its own level of informativity depending on the level of the reader. An explanation of oxygen like *Oxygen is a gas* may be considered as rather a banal comment by certain text users because of their acquired knowledge of the subject. The receiver's "real world" or *the socially dominant model of the human situation and its environmental constituents* (Beaugrande & Dressler, 1981:146) co-ordinate and place the perception of facts. If the text were to be extended by the addition of *...it is a chemical element without colour, taste or smell, present in the air and necessary for all forms of life on earth and is necessary for the process of burning. The symbol for oxygen is O.* the text informativity is increased and also the likelihood of its acceptability by rather more sophisticated readers.

5.3.4 Intertextuality

Another factor that complicates acceptability is the use of well-established beliefs that are so ingrained in our thinking that we use them as a yardstick in judging fundamental issues. Such beliefs may prove to be obstructive in the perception of text. In communication both producer and receiver depend on previous experience to pass on information. Failure to appreciate shared linguistic and socio-cultural characteristics may impede the acceptance of a particular text. We can illustrate this with the following.

Text 27
Mahmood went to sleep and for two hours he didn't sing anything. If I wanted, I could have sung with the two Rafis, the two well-bound Rafis. I could have sung "At the barricades we'll meet, at the barricades we'll raise liberty aloof through blood and fire." That used to be my song, but I've had it with liberty. Blood and fire. Blood and fire we got, but we're short on liberty (Kenan, 1986:51)

The song referred to in Text 27 is a popular Palestinian revolutionary song. The reception process is controlled by an awareness of the situation of Palestinians and Israelis contesting the same piece of land, of a day-to-day routine of bombing, fighting, humiliation and oppression. Moreover, *but I have had it* has historical relevance. Without the knowledge of dominant Palestinian and Israeli tiredness and depression resulting from a long, long battle, the reader would miss the poignant picture conveyed by Kenan.

5.4   Poetry

With regard to literary texts, and poetry in particular, there is an issue centring around "meaning". This issue concerns the reader in general and the translator in particular. With poetry the translator must transfer the meaning of language which has no limits and is characterised by a unique constructive power. In literature the writer conceptualises and maps out the world in special ways. Each individual map is inimitable whether in the source language or the target language. Each work of art is unique. Each translation of a piece of literature adds to a craft which enhances the humanity of humans. Steiner (1975:XV) attests that *Winckelmann does not erase or replace Aristotle: Coleridge does not render Dr Johnson obsolete; T.S. Eliot on Shelley cannot invalidate Mathew Arnold.*

Let us now go on to examine this point with a brief look at what poets do with words. Words are the instrument of poets. They use them to formulate their texts in a unique way in a variety of forms. Poetic writings, as we saw with regard to literature in general in Chapter One, go beyond the surface, referential meaning. In a good poem words are fresh and vivid and at their very best go beyond conventional use. There is no set of rules to control the way in which a poet uses words.

Discrete words or images may carry their own immediate values but in association with the other parts they hold special artistic value.

The smaller units are inseparable parts of a whole work of art. Word after word, image after image, part after part, all enhance the meaning of the whole.

The poet's aim is to make an impact on the reader. With words poets create beauty or maybe shocking reality. It might be an imitation of the real world, an assemblance of fragments of real life or it may be totally novel, outside the sphere of our knowledge. Whatever the case, each poem presents a unique and unprecedented experience. For instance, T.S. Eliot could distil the knowledge of the world and reformulate it in something like:

Here is no water but only rock

Rock and no water and the sandy road
The road winding above the mountains
Amongst the rock one cannot stop or think
Sweat is dry and feet are in the sand
If there were only water amongst the rock
Dead mountain mouth of carious teeth that cannot spit
Here one can neither stand nor lie nor sit
There is not even silence in the mountains
But dry sterile thunder without rain
There is not even solitude in the mountains
But red sullen faces that sneer and snarl
From the doors of mud cracked houses
If there were water
And no rock
If there were rock
And also water
And water
A spring
A pool among the rock
If there were the sound of water only
Not the cicada
And dry grass singing
But the sound of water over a rock
Where the hermit-thrush sings in the pine trees
Drip drop drip drop drop drop drop
But there is no water

Eliot says in a note that this describes Christ's journey to Emmaus after the Resurrection *but the essential significance lies in it being also a journey through the Waste Land, the modern world as perceived by the poet* (Coombes, 1963:60).

The poet depicts a total image out of a number of simple images. According to Coombes (ibid:60), although there was no attempt at complex development in any of it, *out of the simple material he creates his landscape which is the embodiment of the feeling of barrenness, longing, weariness.* Whether we feel it presents a picture of barrenness, longing or weariness or all of these concepts together or whether it presents a wide spectrum of symbolism, such paraphrasing or clarification falls far short of what Eliot intends. The total image assimilates different images, different kinds of experience and thought to form an organic unit of expression.

We enjoy a literary work of art in the way we enjoy a pattern – a musical pattern, a sculptured pattern, a painted pattern, a word pattern. A pattern is characterised by being unique and by evoking a holistic effect. Any message or moral is difficult to grasp since the expression is an organic unity by which the poet intends to create an effect. This presents serious difficulty for readers and translators of poetry. In general, readers and listeners seek to isolate the meaning of a stretch of language which consists of arbitrarily selected words or conventionalised signals. The problem in poetry, however, as Steiner (1975: 253) puts it, is that *the welding of matter and form is so close that no disassociation is admissible.*

5.5 Conclusion

We have stressed the fact that a speaker/writer tries to bring about a textuality that will satisfy the listener/reader. An effort is made to ensure that a piece of language is communicative. A listener or reader works on the *closely-knit patterns of grammatical dependencies and syntax* which *are major signals for sorting out meanings and uses* (Beaugrand & Dressler, 1981:49 & 3) and help text users to decipher meaning. The task is not easy if the concepts expressed, whether real-world or fictitious, are outside the experience of the receiver. In transactional language it is more likely that we can get to a full meaning in a straightforward manner. When complexities are introduced, however, despite attempts at acceptance and a desire to reach a compromise, shades of meaning are lost. Possible causes for this have been suggested as the intricacies of the spoken mode, complexities of textual cohesion and coherence, excesses of negotiation, difficulties in interpreting the intention of the writer/speaker, density of information and lack of prior knowledge. The extreme case of complexity is represented by the work of the poet who employs words to transfer something beyond meaning, to create a unique artistic effect.

The following two chapters will now go on to deal with implications for the translator of dealing with meaning at a level deeper than the surface. They will examine how texts may mean more than they apparently express literally. An attitude towards the translation of poetry will be suggested, indicating the type of person who is qualified to translate it and how a translator might go about dealing with its intricate nature.

Chapter Six

Translating Beyond the Norm

6.1   Equivalence

In the process of translation, problems are likely to arise in conveying information from the source language to the target language. A skilled translator, familiar with the internal aspect of language as a context free code, must cross to the external aspect of what language is for. Skilled translators accept the intentions embedded in a source text and, in their turn, play a special role in transferring those intentions to readers in the target language whose culture will be different.

Concepts in one language are not identical to concepts in another. Each language arranges its "real world" differently and, for Steiner (1975:xiv), each language maps the world differently. These differences pose particular difficulties for learners and translators. One immediate and persistent problem for translating is thus one of equivalence- that is, items that are "semantically and functionally the same" (Chalker &Weiner; 1994:138)

Care needs to be taken when talking about equivalence within the context of translation as it might imply that there is some maximum that can be achieved with regard to equivalence. Complete equivalence is, however, neither possible in one language nor across languages. If, for instance, we consider the English pairs generous – extravagant; slim – thin; valuable-expensive we find that each pair has something in common and is partially synonymous. They have similar denotations but different connotations. Emotional and attitudinal factors must be considered when deciding what the writer or speaker means. This is of special importance for the translator. For instance, extravagant with his words and generous with his words could both be translated into Arabic as مسرف في ألفاظه . This does not, however, distinguish between a different emphasis for extravagant and generous. In context the former, related to "exorbitant", "immoderate", "exceeding normal restraint", might perhaps have a derogative sense and = "over the top in his praise" or "too fulsome in his praise". The latter, however, might imply that a person gives freely and, therefore, = "kind in what he said". In such a case the translator might provide a more accurate translation – سخي في تعبيراته [generous in his expression]. The choice, of course, depends on the context and situation. In this respect as Bassnett (1980:14-15) explains

> *Even apparent synonymy does not yield equivalence, and Jacobson shows how intralingual translation often has to resort to combination of code units in order to fully interpret the meaning of single unit...Since each unit contains within itself a sense of non-transferable associations and connotations.*

A major source of complexity in language is the putting together of elements to form an intricate and composite structure. Sophistication in language comes from a build up of discrete items to form a text. It is not only the accumulation of words that manifests sophistication but also significant is the build up of the "fuzziness" of meaning. Fuzziness results from the relationship between words themselves and what they stand for and those who use them. Beaugrande & Dressler (1981:85) believe that many concepts are so adaptable to differing environments that they remain quite fuzzy in regard to their components and boundaries. They (ibid:87) suggest that

> *The fuzziness and instability of concepts and their possible components should become steadily less prominent when they appear in more and more determinate contexts of communications. In that perspective, the sense of an expression or the content of a concept are definable as an ordered set of hypotheses about accessing and activating cognitive elements within a current pattern.*

6.1.1 Collocation

Newmark (1981:114) explains that a collocation is the element of system in the lexis of language. Baker (1992:285) expresses the same concept as "the tendency of certain words to co-occur regularly in a given language". The Oxford Dictionary of English Grammar more precisely says that it is a type of construction where particular nouns, adjectives, verbs or adverbs form predictable connections with each other" e.g. break off an engagement. Thus collocation consists of two or three words linked together and accepted in the source language. These words belong to the same semantic field and they become collocations only when they are arranged syntagmatically (ibid. 114). Let us, for instance, consider the following examples of collocation as the basis of our discussion.

1. rise and shine   صحصح وفوق
2. work hard   يعمل بجد
3. strong tea   شاي ثقيل
4. a tall tree   شجرة عالية
5. high heels   كعوب عالية
6. high speed   سرعة عالية
7. a bunch of keys   مجموعة مفاتيح/سلسلة مفاتيح
8. fish and chips   سمك وبطاطس مقلي/بطاطس مقلي وسمك
9. a pinch of salt   قليل من الملح/قبصة ملح
10. slim body   رشيق
11. thin body   نحيف

With regard to the above examples, rise and shine is a British catch phrase. The use of an Arabic catch phrase in translation is appropriate as it conserves the colloquial nature of the expression.

The other examples allow for a translation that is a straightforward collocation. It would be odd if the translator were to use exact literal equivalents.

• In Arabic the back translation of strong tea is heavy tea.

- Tall tree would seem strange as, in Arabic, tall is an adjective used of people rather than objects like trees. In Arabic a tree is high.

- A back translation of a bunch of keys is a set of keys. Another back translation is a chain of keys referring to the whole bunch, something that is not appropriate in English.

- In English the expression is fish and chips. It is not normal to say chips and fish while in Arabic the order does not matter.

- A pinch of salt could be translated as قليل من الملح/حفنة ملح. The rarely used Arabic collocation قبصة ملح is closer in meaning and حفنة ملح a back translation of a handful of salt gives the impression of a larger amount of salt and might give inaccurate sense. Slim and thin when referring to the body have clear denotations and have a defined Arabic equivalent. Used with different collocations, however, this is not so – slim could mean رشيق and thin نحيف, but note, slim hope/chance أمل ضعيف/فرصة ضعيفة, vanished into thin air إختفى في الهواء, thin population كثافة سكان قليلة, thin audience حضور قليل.

A translator must therefore be familiar with collocations in both the source language and the target language. Newmark (1981:116) believes that collocations are the lexical tramlines of language and he suggests not only to follow but also to break them (going off the tramlines) when they are broken in the source language text.

The examples discussed so far illustrate the fact that a word is a lexical unit. It has a discrete linguistic value of its own. When it works within a linguistic system it acquires a complexity of lexical meaning. Baker, (1992:12) explains that the lexical meaning of a word or lexical unit may be thought of as the specific value it has in the particular linguistic system and the "personality" it acquires through usage within the system. The way language works does not allow for successful analysis of meaning with regard to a discrete word, pattern or structure. It is very difficult, therefore, to provide guidelines for handling different types of non-equivalence among languages. The present writer would suggest that it is the choice of the translator that matters. The translator employs and directs the linguistic system of the target language relying on understanding the way the producer of the source language employs the linguistic system. Since it is impossible to achieve a complete equivalence, "adequacy" then, serves the purpose, Hatim & Mason (1990:8) suggest that adequacy of a given translation procedure can be judged in terms of users' needs.

There are further demands made on translators in their role as mediators. They must deal with elements of meaning that go beyond the propositional meaning. For instance, let us consider The army is the shield of the nation – الجيش درع الأمة. The word shield refers to the variously shaped and sized detached pieces of armour made of leather, wood or metal which serve to receive and ward off a thrust or stroke from an enemy weapon. The elongated form large enough to cover most of the body is a description that is applied under normal circumstances. In The army is the shield of the nation, however, shield and nation do not normally go together in this way. The norm is violated for the purpose of bestowing attributes beyond the limit of each word taken separately. A translator must look into such attributes and highlight them.

In order for translators to perceive attributes beyond the norm they must be aware of the principal of functional variation, or register (Halliday, 1985:44). For Halliday, register is related to dialect and dialect indicates the particular place and group to which a person belongs. As Halliday puts it, members of a speech community recognise a typical configuration (ibid: 44). The functional variety is determined by "field" (what is going on), "tenor" (who is taking part) and "mode" (the role the language is playing). Awareness of the way language varies has two major implications. First, the translator can identify the most appropriate meaning of a particular word directed by the field of discourse involved and, hence, make an adequate choice. A word like court has different meanings according to the context involved – a building, tennis or the law. It is, therefore, part of the translator's task to have different expectations about what kind of language is appropriate to a particular situation (Baker, 1992:16). Second, the translator must spot fuzziness in meaning in the source language and try to eliminate it when searching for an equivalent in the target language.

6.1.2 Suggested Strategies

The initial discussion here will be about strategies for dealing with equivalence in a restricted word for word sense. Later in the chapter, however, the implication of equivalence will be considered with regard to some example texts. Baker (1992:26) suggests the five strategies indicated below for dealing with lack of equivalence rising from the fact that languages are different from each other. To transfer from one language to another is to alter the *forms which cannot but fail to coincide totally. There is no absolute synonymy between words in the same language, so why should any one be surprised to discover a lack of synonymy between languages.* (Bell, 1991: 6)

(a) Translating by a more general word (super-ordinate): This strategy is helpful when the target language has no direct meaning. It is also useful for dealing with non-equivalence in the absence of propositional meaning. It can work since *the hierarchical structure of semantic fields is not language specific (Baker: ibid.).* For instance, a virtual state of war exists between the two countries might be translated ما هو قائم بين البلدين أشبه ما يكون بحالة حرب. English (the source language) uses the abstract *virtual* which does not exist in Arabic (the target language). The word *virtual* certainly expresses a concept in

Arabic but there is not a definite equivalent. The translator has no alternative but to use a general expression – أشبه ما يكون "more like".

Words that cause problems of this type are mostly culture specific. For instance, the word حديث used in a religious context is translated as "tradition" by professional translators. Sometimes they transliterate and use hadith which, in fact, means "talk" (i.e. the talk of the Prophet Muhammed).

(b) **Translating by a more/less expressive word:** In the following conversation

> A: I don't see how I can help
> B: You have a car.
> A: Yes. A car and an ass too.
>
> (Kenan,1986:18),

the word ass means حمار but the whole utterance A car and an ass too can be translated سيارة وحمارة. In English an ass may be male or female, but there is a slightly more expressive meaning in Arabic in the use of حمارة (*humara* = "female ass"). The use of this form is a felicitous one for several reasons. It is an everyday word with which Arab readers are familiar and such familiarity is likely to generate intimacy between reader and text. The use of a distinctive gender is a delicate touch in that حمارة (*humara*) rhymes with سيارة (*sa'yara* = "car"). This is likely to make a greater impact on the reader or hearer in the target language. They will enjoy the music of the rhyme and the fun when they are particularly familiar with the use of gender in this specific situation.

(c)   Translating by cultural substitution: A translation of الشذوذ الجنسي from Arabic into English as sexual perversion would reflect how much the expression is emotionally loaded. Mona Baker (ibid :24) believes that such a translation is *inherently more pejorative and would be quite difficult to use in a neutral context without suggesting extreme disapproval.* A less expressive term, such as for instance, *homosexuality,* is required when the target language is English. This example illustrates what might be called cultural substitution and entails translating a word which does not have the same propositional meaning into a culture-specific word.

The same is true of the term *lesbian* مساحقة or *lesbianism* سحاق. The words are derived from the root سحق which means in English *"crush", "suppress", "destroy".* A derivative is سحقا *"become remote or damned".* It reflects strong disapproval. To translate from Arabic to something like *this damned, sexual perversion in women* in English would not be appropriate. A neutral term is called for such as المرأة الممارسة للجنس مع مثيلتها.

Another example of how one community might not tolerate certain cultural aspects of the source language is seen in the word crusade which can now be used to mean "a violent campaign". The recent use of the word by George W Bush in a television broadcast is, however, likely to stir strong emotions if interpreted by Arabic speakers in its older meaning as " a Christian campaign" particularly against Moslems.

What captures the attention of individuals or whole communities may be entirely different to the intent of the original. Hence, titles of films and stories are frequently replaced by titles different in meaning from that apparent in the source language. The Patriot, for instance, is translated as *AlBatal -البطل* *(The Hero)* to attract more audience.

(d)   Translating by paraphrase: To illustrate this let us again use the word lesbian. The concept exists in Arabic and the direct equivalent المساحقة/is available. We could, however, use a different translation, because it is not familiar to many people. In this case we might resort to a paraphrase like المرأة الممارسة للجنس مع مثيلتها, the back translation being *a woman having sex with another woman.* When an item like this is semantically complex we can assemble elements of the source meaning to express the concept.

*R*elated elements can be used in paraphrasing the word *Dadaism - الدادية.* Failing to find an equivalent in Arabic, a translator might use the English word with the addition of the determiner ... ال, take away the suffix -ism and replace it with the Arabic suffix ية - to form an Arabic noun. The term "الدادية" is highly specialised and available to only the few who are able to connect the concept with its origin. Failure to clarify its significance might well lead to confusion among the majority. Hence a paraphrase like "مدرسة الدادية في الفن" = *Dadaism, a school of art* is to be recommended. Unless the frequency of a particular word is high in the target language, translation by paraphrase is a suitable technique.

(e)   Translating by omission: Although omission may seem an extreme strategy, it does no harm occasionally to overlook a word if its meaning is not essential. Moreover, this strategy can be effective if too much paraphrase might divert the attention of the reader or hearer in the target language.

Sometimes the meaning of a particular word is implied in the general meaning and translating it would cause unnecessary redundancy. For instance, a suitable Arabic translation of *vanished into thin air* might be اختفى في الهواء [vanished into air]. The Arabic word for *air* implies thinness and, furthermore, there is not an appropriate equivalent in Arabic to replace *thin* in order to give the utterance its exact significance.

Since the main aim of a stretch of language (source text or target text) is to achieve acceptable communication, it is sometimes practical to transfer text into a visual medium. For instance, a picture of "a binate leaf" is much more effective than a translation like ورقة شجر زوجية /النمو. If for any reason a translator fails to find an adequate equivalent in the target language for something that can be depicted visually, this is a useful strategy. This option is especially useful if it is important to keep the target language translation concise.

6.2   Textual Problems

We have so far been concerned with aspects of meaning at the more limited level of word or phrase. When words are put together, however, the interaction between them leads to greater complexity. Thus, we need to examine the intricacies of text where language is more *functional* and is *doing some job* (Halliday & Hasan, 1985:52). It is true that translators must deal with lexico-grammatical patterns and various kinds of individual relations but they also have to discover the structural continuity of a source text. The discussion now needs to shift to problems faced by the translator at textual level making use of issues raised in the previous chapter with regard to intentionality and acceptability.

6.2.1   Speaking and Writing

Translators as mediators need to use their knowledge of the features of language (spoken or written) as well as strategies of achieving intentionality to bring about acceptability. Towards this end the process of translating can be seen as one of decision making.

Chapter Five outlined some of the devices speakers and writers use to get their messages across appropriately in the two different modes. We saw that speakers repeat, backtrack, expand and the like depending on feedback from their listeners. An interpreter must relay a spoken message in a calculated way. If speakers in the source language hesitate and use many sound-fillers to give themselves extra time to organise their thoughts, the translator or interpreter has two options. The choice of one or another will depend on the situation.

If the hearers are merely interested in the content of the stretch of language, the interpreter must cut down on the sound fillers and hesitations. The gist of the message must be transferred to the listeners. This is a very sophisticated strategy. Speakers in the source language use their own ways to facilitate production in order to fulfil acceptability. The intricate role of the translator/interpreter is to decide on the degree of mediation that should be involved. Imbalance might lead to ambiguity if maximal mediation is used and the interpreter says less than is necessary. Conversely, every er and um might be voiced leading to ambiguity by saying too much.

Sometimes the interest of listeners or readers in how things are expressed goes side-by-side with their interest in the content. In this case the interpreter should be very accurate in transferring the ums and ers. The translator of a story or a novel, for instance, should echo the fillers of reluctance and hesitancy. The writer of the source text will have used them to represent a particular mood or attitude. To create an overall picture of what the original writer was trying to depict, they must appear in the translation. Another example of retaining the fillers might occur in a court of law. For instance, a faithful interpreter needs to reflect the hesitancy of the accused because this would help the legal body in making their judgement. In the same context, an aggressive interruption should be expressed by the interpreter indicating exactly how it was made.

Speakers in both source language and translation constantly interpret audience reaction. Both are put under pressure of different sorts. The speaker of the source language might repeat words and ideas in response to audience feedback but the translator has to make a decision as to what to repeat and how far to go in interpreting the mood of the source language speaker and the mode of speaking involved. In the following text cited by Bygate (1987:17), and already referred to in the previous chapter, *South America* is repeated twice and *the young continent(s)* four times as the two participants in the conversation seem to be unable to carry on with ease.

M: in the old – or in the young continents
T: erm the young continent the young continents
M: in the young continent America South America
T: South America

M: near Peru
T: near

A translator would have to decide how many repetitions to include depending on the situation in which the translation was being made.

When a speech or dialogue is to be translated in written form the translator will have to choose between being faithful to the original or abandoning features of the spoken mode which are superfluous to the written form of the language. In Arabic the divergence between spoken and written forms is very wide. This kind of divergence leads to problems with regard to cohesion and coherence. The local spoken dialect of an Arab official, for instance, will diverge from formal written Arabic. Therefore, a written translation into standard Arabic would represent a highly mediated version of the original.

6.2.2 *Implicature*

The notion of "implicature" was considered previously when we discussed the idea that utterances could mean more than what was apparently said. Participants in the source language exert an effort to infer information that might not be explicit. Let us, for instance, consider the following:

A: I don't see how I can help you
B: You have a car.
A: Yes. A car and an ass too.
B: Well, right at the moment I am not looking for asses.

A: Somehow I didn't think you were. Anyway why not? My kingdom for a horse.

B fails to answer A's enquiry and the result is the violation of maxims like "quality" and "relevance". There is, however, recurrent co-operation in spite of this. Translators need to be able to grasp what is implicit so that they can transfer the appropriate inferences. Failure in this regard will short circuit the text. A translator should convey the contributions of both interlocutors so that the result will be acceptable to the listener or reader. Thus, a possible Arabic translation would be

أ- لا أعلم كيف يمكنني مساعدتك.

ب- عندك سيارة ؟

أ- نعم سيارة وحمارة أيضا.

ب- على أي حال حاليا لا أبحث عن حمير.

أ- أدرك بشكل ما أنك لست بفاعل ذلك. ولكن لم لا. أنا شخصيا أبادل مملكتي بحصان.

in which the speaker tries to be sarcastic regarding the availability of car but the enquirer understands the implicit information. Further, both the "quality" and "relevance" maxims are flouted but the co-operation of the interlocutors is obvious.

Apart from being a competent producer of the target language, the translator must be an outstanding reader of the language who can, for instance, scrutinise interlocutors' covert intentions.

In dealing with the question of the degree of mediation acceptable there are no black and white answers. A translator must (as, for instance, already indicated above in 6.1.2.c with regard to translating by cultural substitution) use discretion *as a processor of intentions in any source language text. He must be in a position to make a judgement about the likely effect of the translation on the target language readers/hearers* (Hatim & Mason, 1990:65). Perhaps with regard to our example from the American President's speech (6.1.2), an interpreter in the White House might have more effectively translated Bush's reference to a "crusade" against terrorism in the following way *strong campaign.* Though in a transactional style the picture is relatively clear, the translator of literary or social language has many choices to make depending on the intention of the source text.

6.2.3   *Textuality*

In the previous chapter we discussed factors that might cause a breakdown in textuality. Coherence plays an indispensable role in helping source language receivers to control and consequently accept a text. In their turn, based on their understanding of the similarity and dissimilarity of the systems in each language involved, translators should take account of producing coherent texts in the target language.

In a detailed sense the linguistic resources in each language are unique and an important contribution to coherence comes from cohesion (Halliday & Hasan (1985:48). Translators cannot, however, replicate the system of the source language in the target language because each language has its own system. For instance, the marking of gender in Arabic is not replicated in English. Coherence helps them recognise the logic and special relations within a text. *At any point after the beginning, what has gone before provides the environment for what is coming next. This sets up internal expectations; and these are matched up with the expectations . . . that the listener or reader brings from external sources, from the context of situation and culture* (ibid: 48). For instance, the opening statement (We must hurry) of the following text helps bring coherence to the rest of the text. The relation of the following facts provided explains the need for hurry. Because of the political situation lack of speed might result in there being no one to sign the treaty. Then the final sentence links back to the original statement.

> *"We must hurry," I told our Norwegian friends, "or we may end up with a peace treaty but no government to sign it." We were in Stockholm on 17 August, almost a month after Johan Holst's visit to Tunis. Our coalition looked shakier than ever. The High Court of Justice had ruled that the Shas Party leader, Arye Deri, who was facing charges of financial wrongdoing, must give up his Cabinet seat, even before the Knesset had decided on whether to remove his parliamentary immunity. Meanwhile, further negotiation in Oslo, in the wake of Holst's intervention in Tunis, had whittled down the differences with the Palestinians to just three points. "Let's try to wrap it up now," I urged Holst, "while I am here in Scandinavia."*
> (Peres, 1995:403)

6.2.4 *Situationality*

A translator's processing abilities should enable the analysis of a text and its correlation with a situation since a text has an integral relationship with situation. Awareness of shared knowledge or context sheds light on the intrinsic intentionality of a text. As indicated in the previous chapter, a text *like I'm sorry if I'm er .. shall we go and have a bite .. or have you had your ... Oh, by the way, we can't go in my ...you see, I've failed my ...Ugh, the examiner was an absolute ..* becomes intelligible only when we are aware of the situation – the place (Oxford Circus) and what happened (the man's friend turns up late at lunchtime after failing his driving test). The translator must keep an eye on the text and, if it seems to be too ambiguous, provide some information about the situation. Here, the addition of *(I've failed) my driving test or we can't go in my (car)* or both of them might be helpful. The Arabic translation might thus be أنا آسف إذ كنت قد...هلا ذهبنا لتناول لقمة... لربما تكون قد... آه بالمناسبة لا نستطيع أن نذهب ب(سيارتي) كما ترى.. لقد فشلت في (اختبارالقيادة) اوه كان الممتحن ...جدا.

Another option might be to use footnotes to clarify the Arabic translation.

6.2.5 *Informativity*

Problematic informativity as indicated in Chapter Five puts translators in an awkward situation since they are not the information providers. Thus, when a translator realises that there is too much or too less information, a decision must be made. For instance, when competent translators realise that an audience is being bombarded with excess information they might interfere by redistributing information.

Such interference might take the form of under-translating or over-translating text and it might also be a way of controlling the manner of presentation in order to monitor coherence in the target language. This is a way of accommodating overwhelming complexity such as the organisation of events, arranging sequences to suit the informativity of events and choosing an appropriate text type in the target language – poetic for poetic, scientific for scientific. Thus, the translator plays the role of facilitator.

In terms of a roadside sign, the following piece of text is, for instance, faulty in terms of informativity as well as situationality – Since it is a slippery road we would advise you, motorists in particular, to slow the speed of your vehicles down as soon as possible. Otherwise you will endanger our lives and the lives of other road users. An appropriate translation might cut it down to خفف السرعة - زلج طريق = *Slippery Road Slow Down.* The initial *Slippery Road* is likely to catch motorists' attention indicating the need to slow down because of bad road conditions as reconfirmed by the following statement.

6.2.6 *Intertextuality*

As indicated above, text users rely a great deal on background knowledge. The translator of *The Road to Ein Harood*, referred to in 5.3.4, must relate linguistic and socio-linguistic characteristics - Whose Harood is it? Does it belong to the Palestinians or the Israelis? A special knowledge of the conflict involved helps to achieve some form of acceptability.

It is to be expected that different translators will depend on different intertextuality. In illustration, let us consider some phrases from Text 27 quoted in Chapter Five.

> *Mahmoud went to sleep and for two hours he didn't sing anything. If I wanted, I could have sung with the two Rafis,* ***the two well-bound Rafis.*** *I could have sung say "**At the barricades** we'll meet, at the barricades we'll raise liberty aloft through blood and fire". That used to be my song,* ***but I've had it with liberty.***

For each of the phrases underlined and emboldened we might provide two translations

(1)   *(the two well-bound Rafis)* = *(a)* رافع ورافع

رافع ورافع المكبلان بالأصفاد (b) or المقيدان

(2)   *(at the barricades)* = *(a)* عند الحاجز or *(b)* عند

المتراس

(3)   *(I've had it with liberty)* = *(a)* عييت في نيل

الحرية *or*

(b) مللت

العمل من أجل الحرية

- 165 -

With regard to (1), translation (a) is neutral and does not reflect harassment or oppression, whereas (b) speaks for the anger of the bound Rafis rather than for those doing the binding.

In (2), translation (a) looks at barricades from the point of view of those who are kept in and cannot move freely from one side to the other. Translation (b) reflects a protective measure to guard those behind the barricades.

Finally, in (3) translation (a) gives the impression that someone has worked hard against the odds but has failed because of too much pressure to withstand whereas (b) indicates a boring and maybe unnecessary occupation, with the speaker looking for something more interesting to do.

6.3   Conclusion

It is the translator's role to strike a balance between the language producer's intentions and achieving a textuality that is satisfactory to the listener or reader. Ambiguity and complexities arise when meaning goes beyond the norm represented by transactional language illustrated earlier.

In the transference of meaning from source to target text one persistent problem is that of equivalence and the lack of synonymy between languages. When discrete words are put together they create an intricate structure. This composite structure of units to form a text is another problem for the translator to deal with.

One form of complexity stemming from the build up of words is that of collocation. Here it is suggested that the translator should, when possible, use avoidable equivalents in the target language and, towards this end, should be familiar with collocation in both languages. When elements of meaning go beyond the propositional, we need to maintain adequate transfer. Dependent on the context and situation, strategies for dealing with collocation are translating by a more general word, a more or less expressive word, cultural substitution, paraphrase and omission.

Synthesis leads to structural continuity which gives rise to textual problems pertaining to intentionality and acceptability. In social language speakers use devices like repletion, backtracking, hesitation and expansion, relying on feedback from listeners, and a translator/interpreter has to decide whether to give the gist of a spoken text by purifying it or to voice every detail. Whatever the degree of mediation decided on, the view taken here is that it must take account of

- the importance of reflecting implicature
- preserving textuality which supports intelligibility
- balancing the amount of information
- discerning socio-linguistic characteristics
- deciding whether to remain neutral according to the situation.

Chapter Seven

Towards Learning to Translate Beyond the Norm

7.1   Introduction

The previous chapter outlined some features of language beyond
the transactional norm that are likely to present the translator with
a range of choices and suggested some possible solutions. Now
the concern of what follows is to offer some practical suggestions
for how the awareness of the trainee translator might be raised
with regard to some aspects of how such subjective language
works. McEldowney (1992) approaches the problem for language
learners by an initial focus on the adjectival system in English.

7.2   Adding Subjectivity to Text

In her various writings McEldowney points out that there are
essentially two broad adjectival functions. An adjective might
have the purpose of assigning items to generally accepted classes
or types. Thus in

> *In a steamer chair, under a manuka tree that grew in the
> middle*
> *of the front grass patch, Linda Burnell dreamed the
> morning away.*
> (Mansfield, 1922)

we find a type of chair, a type of tree, a type of patch referred to. That is, Linda sat in a steamer chair rather than a kitchen chair, a dining chair, an easy chair; she was under a manuka tree rather than a Kauri tree, a peach tree, a lemon tree; she was on a grass patch rather than a patch of concrete, or shingle or dirt. Such usage belongs to the transactional language dealt with in the earlier chapters of this book and is best mastered before language learners and trainee translators move on to more subjective language.

McEldowney points out that a more subjective use of adjectives is significant in literature and other types of more personal writing. To show how this works she provides the following two texts:

(A) *It was a beautiful early evening and the green of the grass was a soft deep colour. The golden light came through the copper beech and the cedar showed the lines of its beauty against a soft pinkish-golden sky.* (Christie, 1991:108)

(B) *It was early evening. The grass was green. The sun shone through the leaves of the copper beech trees. The cedar was silhouetted against the sky which was streaked with pink and gold.* (McEldowney, 1992: 15)

Text (B) is an essentially factual description of the scene. There is no attempt to make a special effect of any sort. It describes merely what an impartial observer would see. In contrast Text (A) provides an interpretation of the scene beginning with the subjective adjective *beautiful* to signal how the reader should view the scene. The writer then goes on to describe what made the evening beautiful in her eyes. This is done with constant modification of the nouns:

- The grass was not merely green but the green of the grass was *soft* and *deep*.

- The rays of the sun did not merely shine through the leaves of the beech tree but *golden* light cam through the *copper* beech. (Even though *copper* is here essentially a classifier it is also being used to help paint a "colourful" picture – gold against copper; gold and copper against soft deep green; all against soft pinkish gold.)

- The cedar was not merely silhouetted against the sky but it *shows its beauty* against a *soft pinkish-golden* sky.

McEldowney argues that

> *Buried in the passage is a basic core, "uncoloured" meaning – an early evening scene. To explain the epithet[7]* beautiful *with regard to this scene various devices are used, among which are other epithets, to make an effect, to play on the reader's imagination; to make the reader see not just an evening scene but to see the beauty of the scene as it appears to the writer. It might be suggested that, to appreciate the beauty being described, the reader must also be aware, no matter how subconsciously, of the "uncoloured" description inherent in the implied contrast.* (McEldowney, 1992:16)

---

[7] That is, a subjective adjective as opposed to a "classifier" of non-subjective adjective.

The same scene might be described in other terms – perhaps as *dreary* or *frightening* or *creepy* or *damp*.

-

7.2.1  *Try This (8)*

Colouring a Scene

To understand how the system works,

1.　　colour Text (B) above to become

　　(i)　*dreary*

　　(ii)　*frightening*

➡ *Now turn to the KEY.*

2.　(i)　translate the original uncoloured text (B) into Arabic

　(ii)　write a *dreary* description of the scene in Arabic

　(iii)　write a *creepy* description of the scene in Arabic

→ *Now turn to the **KEY**.*

As one tool in learning to produce and translate non-transactional language, McEldowney suggests that it is important to build up a facility in moving backwards and forwards between stark, transactional language and "coloured" language, providing a range of different effects in the way illustrated. Such experimentation helps build up an awareness of more creative language in both source and target languages. As will have been discovered from the task in 7.2.1 above, however, the activity suggested requires a degree of sophistication with language that might not be at the immediate command of the trainee translator. A judicious use of transition notes (4.2.2) can be of great help here.

7.3 Using Transition Notes to Deal with Colour

As we saw in Chapter Four transition notes can be developed to control the level of grammatical sophistication appropriate to the individual learner. They can similarly control the level of colour or lexical sophistication involved.

7.3.1 A Prose Example

McEldowney (1992.17) provides the following text to illustrate how transition notes can help the trainee in developing a facility with "coloured" language:

> *His father, having freshened himself at the well they shared with their neighbours, had also donned sleeping trousers and jacket and had sunk into his deck chair on the back veranda as he was in the habit of doing every evening to gaze out over the small garden.*

Among the bamboo fences on either side there grew a few melati bushes and one or two banana and papaya trees. Beyond the garden was the river. On the other bank, partly hidden by the bamboo and by the banana trees and tall coconut palms was the kampong.

The short tropical night was falling and men and women were coming down the slippery, cracked loam slope to cleanse themselves in the river for the night. After their baths, the younger men would stay behind for a while, squatting as they smoked their native cigarettes, laughing and chatting and looking at the girls and younger women who had remained behind to wash a sarong or rinse cooking utensils. Naked children dived and splashed about, ducking each other roughly, balancing on a floating tree trunk and filling the stillness of the evening with their shrill cries of joy.

She points out that the first paragraph might be entitled "The Father" and is a narrative (2.2.2) of the father's behaviour 'then', on the specific occasion being related. We are also told that sequence happens habitually as marked by *as he was in the habit of doing every evening*. The narrative sequence is outlined by the relatively sophisticated dynamic verb forms *having freshened, had put on, had sunk, to gaze* in which the form *having freshened* embeds a step in a non-finite *after* clause and *to gaze* embeds another in a non-finite clause of purpose. If this sequence were to be related in **grammatically** core form (4.3), we would find something like:

1.   freshened   himself

2.	donned	his sleeping trousers & jacket
3.	sank	into a deck chair
4.	gazed	across the garden

Then if it were to be reduced to **lexically** core or "uncoloured" form we might find:

1.	washed	himself
2.	put on	his pyjamas
3.	sat down	
4.	looked	across the garden.

The second paragraph of the text might be entitled "The Garden" and is a stative description (2.2.3) as marked by the stative verbs *grew* and *was*. As is common with description related to narrative it takes on the reference of the narrative – in this case 'then', on that occasion and also implied is 'on other occasions'.

Appropriate grammatically, uncoloured core notes might be:

what	*where*
the fences	on each side
a few bushes	among the fences
a few trees	among the fences
a river	beyond the garden
some bamboo	on the other bank
some trees	
some palms	
the village	beyond the trees & bushes

in which local reference to the types of trees and bushes involved and the village have been neutralised.

The third paragraph of the text, which might be entitled "The River", is divisible into two sections. The first of these sections is related to 'then' and involves

> *The short tropical night was falling and men and women were coming down the slippery, cracked loam slope to cleanse themselves in the river for the night....Naked children dived and splashed about, ducking each other roughly, balancing on a floating tee trunk and filling the stillness of the evening with their shrill cries of joy.*

It is also descriptive, but unlike the previous section which describes the garden by means of its boundaries and not its contents leaving the reader with an awareness of calm and stillness, this section describing the river concentrates on many people and their activities. The transition from one type of stative description to the other is marked by the use of the dynamic adjective *falling* to describe the night (rather than the more neutral narrative step *night fell*). This is followed by a high proportion of other –*ing* forms together with the lexically full *dived* and *splashed* to describe actions. Grammatically core and lexically uncoloured notes might be:

who	*activity*	*where*
some men & women	coming	down the slope
some children	diving splashing ducking balancing	in the river

	crying out	

The other part of the river description from *After their baths* to *rinse cooking utensils* is marked by *would* as referring both to 'later' and 'habitually'. This is also a description of activity:

who	*activity*	*where*
some younger men	squatting smoking laughing chatting laughing	on the bank
some girls & younger women	washing rinsing	in the river

What is represented by the grammatically core and lexically uncoloured notes related to each section of the text leads to an "understanding" of the central meaning of the text. Let us consider how the writer has taken us beyond this in the way he chose to communicate the information.

7.3.2   Comparing Core with a Coloured Original

It would seem that the father is of a higher social status than the other people referred to in the text and that he belongs to a different (probably governing) culture. When we compare the core and coloured father narrative above, we note that the "coloured" narrative 'heightens' the father's actions to something above the norm – normal people *wash, put on, sit down* and *look* but the father *freshens, dons, sinks down and gazes*. Further, a comparison of the father's washing habits with those of the other people described puts them into an inferior position seen through the father's eyes. We note that the father merely needs to *freshen* himself but the other people do not merely have to *wash* themselves but they must go as far as *cleansing* themselves – the difference, perhaps between an individual who does not engage in any sort of manual work and those who do. The father uses a well shared by a few neighbours while the whole village (*kampong*) must use the river not only for washing themselves but also their clothes and cooking utensils.

This apparent difference in status is further marked by the organisation of the information represented by the different sets of transition notes illustrated in the previous section. We note that the father is cut off from all the life and activity and noise of the river as he sits alone on his veranda. He is cut off from the village by the no-mans-land of his garden with the intervening boundary of trees and bushes on his side of the river and the river itself.

There is a great deal more that can be drawn from the text in this comparison between the coloured and uncoloured version of the information. Ultimately, in the interpretation involved the individual's reactions and perceptions will vary according to experience and expectation. The point is, however, that such comparisons lead the trainee translator to a deeper awareness of the meaning of a source text and the implications for the best possible translation.

7.3.3 Towards Translation

The type of exercise indicated above in 7.2 can be introduced with the help of transition notes. Towards this end a straightforward rendering of the original can be produced from the transition notes outlined above in 7.3.1 to read something like:

> *The father washed himself at the well, put on his pyjamas, sat down and looked across the garden.*
> *The garden had a fence on each side and there were bushes and trees growing in the fences. There was a river at the end of the garden.*
> *Beyond the garden men and women were walking towards the river. There were children in the river. They were diving, splashing, ducking each other, balancing on logs and crying out.*

Learners can then be asked to make appropriate notes about a similar person and surroundings. For instance, McEldowney (1992:34) quotes a group of learners who used the pattern to produce the following:

The chieftain	put on	his cloak	
	walked		down the hall
	climbed		on to the
platform			
	looked		across the
hall			

An intervening space defined by boundaries:

The Hall

what	where
the walls	on either side
some animal skins	on the walls
some spears	among the skins
a car park	beyond the hall

An active scene beyond "no-mans-land":

The Car Park

who	activity		where
some warriors	approaching shaking chanting	their spears	
some women	watching clapping	their hands	
some children	running shouting		around the warriors

These notes adhere to the overall structure of the original text in such a way that learners are made aware of how textual coherence was developed and gives them an opportunity to practise the pattern for themselves. An English text developed from the notes would be something like:

> *The chieftain put on his cloak, walked down the hall, climbed onto the platform and looked across the floor.*
> *The walls on each side had some animal skins on them and there were some spears among the skins. There was a car park outside the hall.*
> *Beyond the hall, warriors were approaching across the car park, shaking their spears and chanting. Some women were watching the warriors and clapping their hands. Some*

children were running around the warriors and chanting.

Students produce an Arabic version of the notes and then produce the text. Now a suitable framework has been established learners can be asked to provide appropriate coloured words for the chieftain on analogy with the example of the father. So for the father we had:

"uncoloured"	*"coloured"*
washed	freshened
put on	donned
sat down	sank
looked	gazed

and, next to the uncoloured words for the chieftain, the second column below indicates coloured English words while the third indicates coloured Arabic words, both sets of coloured words being appropriate to the context of the rest of the chieftain passage.

"uncoloured"		*"coloured"*	
put on	إرتدى	shrugged on	أسبل ردائه على كتفيه
walked	سار إلى	strode	ذرع المكان
climbed	تسلق	leapt	وثب إلى أعلى
looked	نظر	glared	حملق

Such a task directs learners' attention to the effect that can be achieved by using a different register of lexis. Trainee translators need to develop such a facility in both source and target language.

7.3.3.1 ✍ *Try This (9)*

Changing Characters

Two other characters to fit the frame indicated by the original text about the father might be:

The Grandmother		The Burglar	
walked	سار إلى	came	قدم
sat	جلست	opened	فتح
picked up	إلتقطت	went	ذهب
looked	نظرت	looked	نظر

which provide uncoloured words in English and Arabic for the first paragraph.

1.   (i)   Use the words above to write an uncoloured first paragraph about the

grandmother. Write an English version and then an Arabic one.

(ii)   Write transition notes, first in English and then in Arabic, for paragraph 2 about "an intervening space defined by boundaries" and paragraph 3 about "an active scene beyond no-mans-land".

Follow the tables above in 7.3.3 about the father
and the chieftain.

(iii)   Use your notes to write about the grandmother in
English and Arabic

➡ *Now turn to the **KEY**.*

2.   Carry out the same procedure with regard to the
burglar both in English and Arabic. (Remember the
burglar verbs for the first paragraph are given above).

➡ *Now turn to the **KEY**.*

3.   The first two columns below provide the uncoloured
words you have already used. The second two columns
provide a possible coloured word to replace *walked* for
the grandmother and *came* for the burglar. Complete each
coloured column in English and Arabic with suitable
verbs.

The Grandmother
walked   سارت إلى   **doddered**   **تقدم بوهن**

sat
picked up
looked

The Burglar
came   قدم   **crawled**   **تسلل زاحفا**
opened

went
looked

 *Now turn to the **KEY**.*

 *Now turn to the **KEY**.*

- -
- - - - - - - - - - - - - -

Once tasks like those above have been completed learners might be asked to choose an adjective to describe each of the characters developed. For instance:

the father	*the chieftain*	*the grandmother*
the burglar		
freshened	shrugged	doddered
crawled		
donned	strode	lowered
slid		
sank	leapt	fumbled for
crept		
gazed	glared	peered
peeped		
↓	↓	↓
↓		
autocratic	**arrogant**	**infirm**
furtive		

Translate into Arabic.

In this way learners can be led to an awareness of what effect different lexical choices can have on a piece of writing and be led to develop a skill in both source and target languages in this respect. This can be achieved initially by identifying the 'core' information (grammatically and lexically) in a piece of non-transactional language with the help of appropriate transition notes and then comparing it with a range of stylistic variants.

7.4   Towards Poetry

Our examples above related to prose can be seen to provide a step on the way to translating poetry. We will see in the following chapter that translating poetry is an act of deconstruction and reconstruction. Towards this end, in the classroom context, it is necessary to analyze a poem and, in the initial stages, transition notes can be very helpful. An example with regard to Wordsworth's daffodils, the first stanza,

> *I wandered lonely as a cloud*
> *That floats on high o'er vales and hills,*
> *When all at once I saw a crowd*
> *A host, of golden daffodils*
> *Beside the lake, beneath the trees*
> *Fluttering and dancing in the breeze.*

can be represented in simple, uncoloured notes in the following way:

(Wordsworth)   went   for a walk   alone

| | saw | some flowers | |

$\Downarrow$

number	colour	position	action
a lot	yellow	by the lake under the trees	moving

which indicates that the central, core meaning is something like
"Wordsworth went for a walk by himself and saw a lot of yellow
daffodils moving under the trees by the lake." This provides the
basic framework in which students can begin to analyze the poem
and appreciate the effect of Wordsworth's language. For instance,
the core description of the flowers can be matched with
Wordsworth's lexical choices:

"uncoloured"	verse 1
(some flowers)	some daffodils
(a lot)	a crowd
	a host
(yellow)	golden
(by the lake)	beside the lake
(moving)	fluttering
	dancing

This provides the basis for examining the way in which the
description is heightened by the choice of lexis and the similes
suggested and ultimately leads trainee translators to provide
Arabic notes and an Arabic version of the poem – albeit, initially,

a rather pedestrian translation, as shall be made clear in the following chapter.

Information from the second and third stanzas can be added to the table above to extend the comparison. For instance,

> *Continuous as the stars that shine*
> *And twinkle in the milky way*
> *They stretched in never-ending line*
> *Along the margin of the bay*
> *In thousands I saw at a glance*
> *Tossing their heads in a sprightly dance.*

"uncoloured"	verse 1	verse 2
(some flowers)	some daffodils	
(a lot)	a crowd	continuous
	a host	stretched
		never-ending
		ten
	thousands	
(yellow)	golden	shine
		twinkle
(by the lake)	beside the lake	along the
margin of the bay		
(moving)	fluttering	shine
		twinkle
	dancing	tossing

As we shall go on to see in he next chapter, the translation of a poem is, however, a great deal more complex than the initial step suggested here implies.

Chapter Eight

Translating Poetry

8.1 Introduction

Chapter Six considered the role of the translator as a mediator between a non-transactional source text and the recipient of the target text and Chapter Seven provided a practical tool for introducing such concerns to language learners and trainee translators who, at this level, might be one and the same group. Now, this chapter is devoted to the translation of poetry where the concentration is not on informativity but on form. The receiver of a poem is not only concerned with the ideas communicated but also with the way in which they are communicated.

8.2 What is Expected of Poetry

In the broadest sense, there is an expectation that producers of text communicate their intentions as clearly as possible. With regard to poetry, however, that expectation is somewhat modified. We expect poets to convey information and organise their content in such a way that there is often surface ambiguity. With poetry, as we shall see later, the focus becomes a poet's own particular style. In the type of transactional language explored in Chapter Two, personal style is not a central issue. The tendency is, as was seen, to move towards a neutral norm. In Chapter Five it was shown that writers of literature may, from time to time, break away from their individual style to overload a text with information. According to Beaugrande & Dressler, 1981:150), *if this tactic is pursued intensely and often, receivers may become so disorientated that they are unable to utilise a text* and they suggest that it is for this reason that many readers find Joyce's *Ulysses* difficult.

In order to avoid overwhelming complexity language speakers have strategies for arranging the "real" world (fact or fiction) and so do not *experience the world as a bombardment of individual stimuli* (ibid:147) for knowledge leads to further knowledge. As Beaugrande & Dressler explain, this is done in imitation of *a global pattern such as Frame, Schema and Scripts for matching, integrating and controlling large amounts of current materials* (ibid:147). To achieve this, language producers follow techniques of organising the language in order to reveal sequences, situations and events. Textual communication is dependent on the real world. It is the "wellspring" for information, facts, beliefs, cause, effect, logic, structuring and even disorganisation, destructiveness, anarchy and dismantling the real world.

The movement of poets between what conforms to firmly entrenched fact and that which is not fact is unlimited. They feel free to abandon the way facts are organised in our minds and which, in normal situations, are used to control most of the textual world to which we are exposed. There is an apparent violation of what is true for what is false, of what is alive for what is dead. Facts about shape, sound and colour are, for instance, suspended in the following lines by Robert Burns.

> *Oh my luve's like a red, red rose*
> *Newly sprung in June:*
> *Oh my luve's like the melodie*
> *That's sweetly played in tune.*
> (from Crane:1932:1081)

In Burns' special world this woman is an unhealthy colour and is a flower and, further, she is a musical tune, all things which do not balance with our real world knowledge. Suitability and appropriateness are suspended because the poet is creating an imaginary world. This has implications for translators in that they must decide whether to translate literally or to be creative. (See 8.5 below)

In spite of the fact that the worlds created by poets are of their own invention, they are, however, ultimately derived from the real world. The new world cannot be considered grotesque because readers and listeners, especially those with an aptitude to accommodate artistic realities, will find them generally applicable to some real and recoverable context or belief that constitutes their real world. For this reason, it would seem that works of art like sculpture, painting, music, drama and poetry maintain a "virtual reality", an image generated from world reality.

Poetry requires a certain amount of creativity on the part of both the creator and the recipient. Ultimately, novelty is enhanced by means of a certain degree of defiance of the norms of real world textuality. There is, however, a certain degree of predictability with regard to how such defiance represents a transformation of the expected norm. As a result the artistic effect of a work can be examined.

8.3   Artistic Effect

Literary text makes the recipient work. Readers need to be familiar with literary techniques and conventions. A poem, as with any work of art, involves artistic codes that govern the artistic production. Readers need to do more than merely read the words. They need to be trained to grasp predictable and unpredictable codes of reference. It is an act of negotiating with the implicit as well as dealing with uncustomary codes and expectations. It is for this reason that Eagleton (1983:69) says that *to read literature "effectively" you must exercise certain critical capacities.* He also says that the most effective work is *one which forces the reader into a new critical awareness of his or her customary codes and expectation.* (ibid: 68).

Real world codes of interpretation do not usually completely match the codes which govern literary works. Hence, good literary works are meant to inspire as they aim at a sparkling effect, an extraordinary effect, an artistic effect. One of the ways in which the poet achieves artistic effect is by the manipulation of the linguistic code and the recipient must be prepared to distinguish the features of the language of poetry from those of every day language. Also, as already suggested above by the example from Burns, characters, events, places, things are all perceived differently. A beggar in a work of art is not the beggar of the real world. The fly in the real world is not the same as the fly in

> Little fly,
> Thy summer's play
> My thoughtless hand
> Has brushed away.

A poem is a piece of art which must be viewed as a whole.

8.3.1 Artistic Entity

As a creation, a poem, as is the case with any other work of art, is an entity, an organic entity. It makes an effect as a whole. It does not consist of identifiable elements which can be broken down to express their own message. A poem constitutes a unique whole, the inseparable parts of which provide its coherence. The whole is consistent with the special world created by the work.

It is not easy to make an exact, adequate interpretation of a well-constructed poem. Attempts to interpret or paraphrase cannot be regarded as objective accounts of what the poem really is. We cannot expect a definitive "message" from poems and other works of art. Different receptors respond to works of art in different ways. There can be no unanimous, correct interpretation.

In dealing with poetry the recipient is not involved in seeking to discover what the poet means. The purpose is to experience the artistic journey of the poet or the artistic effect. The interest, then, is in what a poem does to us – that is, its artistic effect. So, because there is not a message to extract but an artistic experience to be involved in, a poem is not immune to free interpretation. A wide variety of readings are to be expected and different people will find a completely different significance in the structure represented by a poem.

The idea that a poem does not have a single "correct" meaning or a message waiting to be extracted may lead to some degree of insecurity. This is because of the training most people have in processing real world textuality and the inevitable non-stop linkage of elements of knowledge that occurs within a community. If a driver were to see a road sign like:

> *Slow*
> *Slippery surface*

a host of contexts would interact to lead to an appropriate interpretation. A road sign occurs in a situation which will eliminate certain readings and legitimatise others. In contrast, a poem is not straight forward. At this juncture it is suggested that in dealing with a poem, especially for academic reasons, an appropriate method of proceeding is to analyse it for the purpose of seeing the relations between the structure as a whole and the various elements of its texture. This is intended to help the critic find out how both structure and texture combined in putting forward the poet's experience.

In interpreting a poem, it is necessary to imagine the wide spectrum of factors engaged such as values, beliefs and assumptions which are of purely real world knowledge. Such factors are generated around the work and, in most cases, are not part of the work itself. The poet uses one set of individual codes to formulate an organic unity and the literary interpreter uses infinite codes to decipher the text. Thus, the view taken in this study is that the expected result is the production of a different text. (See for example, the translation of Sonnet 12 in 8.5.2). No matter how the basic sense of the source text is preserved in poetic images or metaphors, paraphrasing and interpreting will remain problematic. There is a paraphrase problem to be dealt with when faced with a metaphor like

Time is out of joint

Oh, cursed spite

That I was born to set right.

Should a paraphrase unfold the hidden metaphorical meaning or should it deal with the surface meaning? If the former, what exactly is the underlying meaning? Hawkes, as cited by Leech & Short (1981:25), says that *metaphor is not fanciful embroidery of the facts. It is a way of experiencing the facts.* A metaphor does not provide literal sense. On the contrary, a metaphor invites readers to make sense beyond the real world functional meaning of the type captured by a paraphrase. With the use of such devices meaning in poetry becomes multi-significant. A poem does not relay a factual message. It is what it is regardless of what accessories paraphrasing and interpreting make every effort to brush it with.

8.3.2   Devices Used for Artistic Effect

Metaphor (defined above in 6.3.1 and below in 8.3.2.3) has been alluded to in our discussion as a device used to bring about artistic effect. Metaphor and other such devices provide for the complexity of multi-faceted meaning and allow the entity of a poem to be self-expressive, a fact that makes interpreting and paraphrasing problematic in the source language. Thus, it is difficult for a translator, whose preliminary task in the process of transferring from one language to another, to use tools which, to some degree, are difficult for users of the source language.

At this point it is essential to identify some of the devices which should not be used for cosmetic purposes or as "fanciful embroidery of the facts" but which should be used for creating a coherent entity that, from beginning to end, evokes a unique "way of experiencing the facts".

As critics, students of literature or translators need to recognise the elements and devices which combine to make a poem an artistic experience. The effectiveness of a literary text is assessed according to how its creator uses words. This does not mean that criticism is the science of assessing how words are used. In fact, it is concerned with values that are normally ignored by science. *We judge a work of art by its effect on our sincere and vital emotion* (Coombes, 1953:8, citing T.S. Eliot). Devices used by poets, then, should be expressive rather than ornamental. Literary appreciation will be to some extent deficient when there is reference to a single discrete element or device without associating it with the whole. We cannot say, for instance, that we know a sonnet by Shakespeare until we have grasped the poem as a whole from beginning to end. Translators must appreciate the form of a poem, be able to analyse its texture in detail, in order to translate it.

With this in mind, let us now, for instance, analyse Shakespeare's Sonnet 12 in order to see how the poet uses poetic devices in an integrative manner for the purpose of creating an effective entity which, in turn, leads to aesthetic enjoyment.

> *When I do count the clock that tells the time,*
> *And see the brave day sunk in hideous night,*
> *When I behold the violet past prime,*
> *And sable curls all silvered o'er with white;*
> *When lofty trees I see barren of leaves,*
> *Which erst from heat did canopy the herd,*
> *And summer's green all girded up in sheaves*
> *Borne on the bier with white and bristly beard:*
> *Then of thy beauty do I question make*
> *That thou among the wastes of time must go,*
> *Since sweets and beauties do themselves forsake*
> *And die as fast as they see others grow,*
> *And nothing 'gainst Time's scythe can make defence*

Save breed to brave him, when he takes thee hence.

The use of the speaker's first person I continues throughout the poem with dramatic effect. The I starts the rising tempo and dominates the whole sequence.

The theme of "sweets and beauties" (l.11) is engaged in complex, poignant forces and events which curtail these very sweets and beauties. The first is the passage of time. It is a *gradually vanishing conceptual entity registered by the poem's aurally and visually ticking* clock (Vendler, 1997:97). Other withering elements are the day fighting the night and losing; the violet fading; the hair becoming grey; the trees losing their leaves; the herd losing its protection from heat; the green of summer becoming dry, brown bundles. All these are fading beauties and the list culminates in the speaker's pondering over the way in which the beauty of the person addressed must go the same way. The inward virtue and outward show (sweetness and beauty), alluded to in the "lofty trees" that protect the herd from heat, are questioned by the speaker.

Three models of death are presented. Time as a form of vanishing is embodied in the first line and carries his scythe in the penultimate line. The first model of death is the decline of what is beautiful and virtuous in life, expressed by adjectives like *sunk, past, silvered, barren,* and culminating in being carried away of a funeral bier. The second model is aggressive and murderous as death takes its victims with *Time's scythe.* The third picture of death depicted is referred to by Vendler (ibid: 98) as *a moral subject. Death now is freely and reflexively elected in response to the sight of a new generation growing up.*

> ..*(sweets and beauties) do themselves forsake*
> *And die as fast as they see the others grow.*

In order to present an exclusive picture, Shakespeare provides a long and varied list of examples. In the first quatrain he was free in the use of verbal quantity to exhibit the examples. In the first three items ("the day", "the violet", "curls") he uses one line for each. In the second quatrain he gives each item ("trees", "summer foliage") two lines. The examples in the first quatrain are presented in their declined state while in the second quatrain, the picture is broader and fuller with the expression of both "before" and "after". The rising tempo enacting the collapse of elements of life requires the use of a repeated linguistic sign in the form of noun + past participle.

These two quatrains are followed by quieter and more solemn movement *(Then of thy beauty do I question make). The horror of the collapse is abated.* The serene march towards the end starts with *Borne on the bier with white and bristly* beard and moves towards *And die as they see others grow*. This is an agonising farewell to a declining generation.

The last couplet represents the moment of illumination. The music is energetic, the words are defiant and the picture is complete. What has been enacted is resolved by an idea that epitomises a counter force to Death - *breed to brave him.*

When we read for appreciation or enjoyment, an analysis of the structure and texture of Sonnet 12 such as that given above may well be irrelevant. Moreover, as already indicated, the theme or content of a work does not explain its artistic values. For instance, according to Muir (1979:45), the theme in Sonnet 12 is that of *urging the young man to marry so as to perpetuate his* beauty or, as he explains later in a different context, it is about how *Time's threat to youth, beauty and even life itself may be countered by the reproduction of the parent in his offspring and by the continuation of the family line*. This knowledge is of little help in enjoying the experience of the development of the theme in the source poem or in presenting the original artistic experience.

Focusing on the theme or on the building of the poem's structure is, however, important for academic purposes. Developing an awareness of poetic structure is conducive to building up knowledge of literary tradition and is also important in teaching the translation of literary works including poetry. The devices used by poets, as we shall see below, make it difficult to preserve the artistic experience in a translation embedded in a poem. It seems important, therefore, to identify the poetic devices involved

8.3.2.1 Rhythm

Verse flows according to a particular rhythm which is more or less controlled and regular. As a rhythm is repeated through the lines of a poem it creates a sense of pattern and the regular beat of Sonnet 12, for instance, speeds us through to the denouement of breeding to defy Death. Rhythm is behind the music of the words. It is an essential characteristic of verse in that it provides for dramatic variety and helps in presenting and reflecting the intention of the poet.

This musical pattern of a poem is a challenge to the translator because such patterns, dependent on the prosody of a source language, are rarely transferable, at least between English and Arabic. A translator, with particular awareness and skills can, however, transform the musical pattern. The transformation pivots around three central issues as will be seen in 8.5 where different translations of Sonnet 12 are discussed.

- The musical pattern can be ignored altogether so that the translation of the poem from one language to another will pay no attention to the music of the original poem.

- A new pattern based on the development of the theme might be composed. This will be an imitation but it will be an imitation of the tempo and momentum of the original. It will rise and fall, become aggressive or abate. Everything is done in imitation of the source experience.

- The source theme, experience and music might be considered to be sources for suggestion. The outcome would be a completely deviant product. It would drift away from or move in parallel with the source poem.

8.3.2.2 Rhyme

Rhyme is another important element in poetry. Where it is used it should be an integral part of the poem. To be effective it must enhance the artistic coherence. Otherwise it is *an empty convention or an affectation* (Coombes, 1953:32). In Sonnet 12, for instance, the rhymes are not ornamental, assembled together with the help of a rhyming dictionary. We can identify the functionality of the words involved when we separate out the final part of each line to see if they collocate in meaning:

> *...barren leaves*
> *...the herd*
> *...girded up in sheaves*
> *...white and bristly beard*
> *...I question make*
> *...time must go*
> *... do themselves forsake*
> *...see others grow*
> *...can make defence*
> *...takes thee hence*

An examination of the above indicates the following

- The utterances work together and nothing is being forced in.
- There is a subtlety in meaning which helps in evoking the feeling of the reader.

- Following rhymes in alternate lines, the rhyming of the final couplet (defence/hence) resolves the meaning neatly and appropriately, underpins the moment of illumination which sheds light on the whole poem.

In translating poetry, obviously, the original rhyming pattern cannot be simply transferred. The choice is either to ignore rhyme or provide a new rhyme system in the target language. If the choice made is to contrive a rhyming system in the target language, it should play a functional role in the artistic coherence of the poem. It might follow the arrangement of rhymes in the source or not. In the latter case translators are free to build a system suitable for their own objectives and creativity which may be affected by the norms of the target language (See 8.5.2 below).

8.3.2.3 Imagery

Imagery carries within itself something which is associated with the other parts of the work to which it belongs. We cannot avoid appreciating the immediate value of imagery separated from the whole but its real value is what it contributes to the whole. As we saw, Sonnet 12 is rich in imagery and our analysis of the development of the poem reveals that the images are an inseparable part of the poem's total expression.

A metaphor can be seen as a reformulation of real world acts, deeds, events and occurrences and represents a major problem for translation. There are no rules for imagery. It cannot be described as "good", "better", "best" but rather as "right", "appropriate", "fitting within a coherent whole" where the images evoked are vivid, suggestive and above all adequate for the writer's purposes. A translator in the process of transferring an organic whole from one language to another must transfer imagery as part of the whole in order to maintain artistic coherence. For instance, Za'rour's translation of Sonnet 12 in 8.5.2 below put imagery together in such a way as to produce a coherent whole though the imagery is somewhat different to that of the original.

In Sonnet 12, the metaphors are not there just for the sake of providing a musical lyric. They accompany the rise and fall of the tempo starting from the clock that tells the time, the brave day devoured by hideous night and continuing until the theme and the music accompanying it abates. Then the poet questions the beauty of the person addressed.

Shakespeare uses metaphor to create original combinations of ideas like trees canopying a herd. Furthermore, elongated complex metaphors are used to develop the concept of death in a multi-dimensional picture - as *summer's green girded up in sheaves, borne on the bier* and with *white bristly beard* is followed by the thought that sweets and beauties must go amongst *the wastes of time* with the whole image being finished in the last couplet as Death *takes thee hence.*

8.3.2.4 Poetic Thought

A poem is a vehicle for poetic thoughts. It could be said that the content of a poem is a thought and such thoughts, as already indicated, do not add to our store of information. They can, however, stimulate our knowledge.

We notice from the way Shakespeare depicts the image of death and cessation of life in *Summer's green girded up in sheaves, Borne on the bier with white and bristly beard* that this is not just a group of images assembled together. In fact they reflect the strong presence of poetic thought, thought which is involved in actively helping to shape the whole expression. The thoughts involved in poems fuse with the recipients' feelings and their sensuous perceptiveness.

Poetic thoughts are an integral part of the poet's work. They extend their roots in the artistic experience. We feel the poet's power when his thoughts are linked and follow the dramatic inevitability of the presentation, setting atmosphere and milieu. In Sonnet 12, Shakespeare plays on the poetic theme of "sweets and beauties". We follow the trend of thought through a number of closely related images. Out of the images the poet creates his panorama of death and defiance of its power.

A literal translator might distort the thoughts transferred because, if a thought is distanced from the poetic milieu, it may well turn out to be banal or less poetic. (See the translation of Sonnet 12 discussed below in 8.5.1) A translator also should keep a thought alive by not dismembering it from the body or the dramatic inevitability of the poem.

8.3.2.5 Feeling

Lack of feeling is death. We enrich our life when we have fresh and profound feelings. Coombes 1953:88) says that *The quality of our living, as human beings, depends very largely on the kind and quality of our feelings, and the quality of our feelings depends partly on our having learned to distinguish true and false feeling, and our readiness to accept for ourselves, when necessary, the readjustment consequent upon such recognition.*

What is so valuable about poetry in particular is that it can reveal hidden or disguised feelings because feelings in poetry are expressed in a way different to the real world. (See the poem about the fly in 7.3) Poetry reveals a common basis of feeling. Whatever intractable feelings we find in ourselves are felt and understood by others – a step towards our emotional and intellectual growth.

Readers of a poem like Sonnet 12 intensify and clarify their feelings because of the way Shakespeare approaches and organises his experience. Such experience deepens, widens and refines our awareness. Shakespeare, the poet, had conflicting feelings about which he thought deeply and the product of the harmonisation of his feelings is his poem. The poet harmonises our feelings by evoking an experience that is individually and sharply felt. It is not personal in the sense that it is produced in a vehement, affirmative and assertive manner. On the contrary,

Sonnet 12 suggests an appropriate emotion in a neutral, impassive way.

The artistic value of poetry is that it helps human beings to be aware of the presence of true and false feelings. Furthermore, it evolves our ability to readjust according to such awareness. When we are exposed more often to feelings of this sort we become better men and women. Whatever approach translators use to a poem, their task is to maintain the experience the source poet tried to evoke. The recipients in the target language have the right to access the original experience of harmonising conflicting feelings as they identify themselves with the hero or heroine.

8.3.2.6 Diction

Diction refers to the vocabulary of a poem, the language of poetry and the different ways of using it. The substantiality, quality and implication of words might fade in ordinary use but in a poetic context they can be revived and recovered. It is part of the work of a good poem to bestow greater precision and suggestiveness on words.

Discrete words are not poetic when they stand outside a poem's context. Take, for instance, *count, clock, time, day, hideous, night, behold, prime* from Sonnet 12. They cannot be considered to belong to specific poetic language. A poet like Shakespeare has the gift of command of language and he uses the words with particular precision, force and effect. He incorporates them in an effective rhythmical expressiveness. For instance, the combinations *..count the clock that tells the time; ...the brave day sunk in hideous night; ...the violet past prime; ...sable curls* are a manifestation of how the poet could form a total ordering of the language. In this poem Shakespeare relies on what is appropriate to the theme. When he speaks about death or the threat of time he uses the expressions *Time's scythe* and *make defence* and when he speaks of defying death he uses *brave him.* They are words of tangible reference organised in a special way to fulfil the writer's ends. Coombes (1953:136-137) explains that words can either be used as symbols for objects or as vehicles for information when they are used without a sense of their active power and he adds the greater the mastery of language that a writer has, feeling the particular precise force and nuance of the words he uses, the more fully and finely can he convey his sense of life, his experience of life felt.

In the source language, diction in a poem is part of a poetic force that reinforces the total effect. A poet gives force to non-poetic words. The rigour of the way the words are put together makes the work transcend normality. The fear is whether it is possible for translators to keep the blend of gracefulness, vigour, vividness of words as worked out by the original poet.

8.4 What Translators Do

All acts of writing and verbal interaction are acts of communication. Poems are composed with the intention of being read or listened to. The poet has the aim of eliciting some sort of response. A poet intends to whet the recipient's appetite. Special devices of the sort referred to above are used for this purpose.

Translators are communicators because they are involved in passing information and artistry from a source language to a target language. Their acts of communication are imposed upon a previous act. The case of translating poetry is a special one because of the involvement of many constraints related, in a very general way, to content and form. Segregation of form and content is, however, also a major constraint for paraphrasers and interpreters in the source language.

A poem should remain an intact artistic experience and a translator, therefore, has a responsibility towards a poem. In handling this responsibility there are three ways of dealing with a translation of a poem. Before discussing them, however, we need to consider what should remain of a source poem in the target language. The most appropriate method of transferring an artistic effect must be considered.

A matter to be addressed is whether translators should transfer the reality of the poem as it is or whether they should interfere, manipulate and modify it. How much interference is tolerable? Should a translator account for missed out or added shades of reality? Poets in the source language use artistic techniques and conventions expecting source language recipients to co-operate and negotiate the challenging code of reference. Is the translator a facilitator? Should the translator be involved in enabling the receiver in the target language to decode expectations?

As mentioned earlier, characters, events, images and linguistic code may be perceived in a different way. This perception has a better chance of becoming absorbed in the source language. When transferred into the target language, however, ambiguity might arise. A translator has limited options in this case and may either interfere or not interfere. Leaving the ambiguity as it is with no interference requires the target language receiver to distinguish obscure features and codes and handle them. Otherwise, translators may be positive facilitators, clarifying, simplifying, reiterating or cancelling when they believe it suitable to do so. Such interference would surely affect the artistic effect as designed by the source poet, something we cannot measure or define accurately in the first place. Interference will, then, derail the planned development and eventually the outcome is a different artistic effect.

As a poem does more than it says, would interference or mere literal transfer from one language to another allow the new work (which is surely not a work of art) to do what the source language meant it to do? This is especially significant in that, as seen above, it is difficult to pinpoint the message or meaning of a poem. Normally, a good work of art is susceptible to abundant interpretations and the artistic experience is multidimensional. So, there is a fear that translation (with or without interference) will not preserve the artistic effect.

In the analysis of Shakespeare's Sonnet 12 above, there
was an attempt to identify the relation between form and content
as well as structure and texture. In a good work of art, form and
content and structure and texture work in collaboration to fulfil an
artistic aim. A translator's task is to work out a similar process
for the fulfilment of similar satisfaction. What is certain is that
there will be some form of satisfaction whether it is similar or
different to the experience acquired from the source language
poem.

8.5 **Methods of Translating**

This section discusses three methods employed by translators and
investigates methodological problems with regard to two
different Arabic translations of Shakespeare's Sonnet 12 and
three different translations of Ruba'iyyat of Omar Khayaam.

8.5.1 *Literal Translation*

The following is a translation by Badr Tawfik from Egypt.

عندما أعد دقات الساعة التي تعلن الوقت
وأرى النهار الشجاع يهوي في الليل المخيف،
عندما أرى ذروة النضج الوردية القديمة
والشعر الأسود المعقوص الذي فضه اللون الأبيض بأكمله ،
عندما أرى الشجر الوفير الثمرات عاريا من الورق،
الذي كان من قبل يظلل قطيع الماشية من الهجير،
وحنطة الصيف وقد طوقت جميعها في حزم
حملها على عربات الحصاد ذو اللحية البيضاء الخشنة الشعر،
هل أستطيع وقتئذ أن أسألك عن جمالك
لأنك لا بد أن تذهب ضمن الذين يضيعون الوقت ،
ما دامت الأشياء العذبة والجميلة تتخلى عن خواصها،
وتموت بنفس السرعة التي ترى بها

الآخرين يكبرون

لا شـئ يصلح للدفاع ضد منجل

سوى النسل الذي يتحداه حين

الترجمة الكاملة لسينوتات)

الزمن

يلبسك الكفن

(شكسبير

(from *Tawfik,* The Complete Translations of Shakespeare's Sonnets)

> [When I count the chimes of the clock that tells the time
> And see the brave day sinks into hideous night
> When I see the old rosy peak of growth
> And the black curled hair completely silvered by the colour white
> When I see the trees abundant with fruit barren of leaves
> Which before shaded the herd from the heat
> The summer's wheat is all girded up in bundles
> Carried on harvest carts by the man with the white bristly beard
> Can I, then, ask you about your beauty?
> Because you must go among those who waste time
> Since sweet and beautiful things forsake their properties
> And die as they see others grow
> Nothing I good enough to defend against time's scythe
> Except to breed to challenge when time dresses you in a shroud.]
> (Translated by Saad, 2002)

This translation is a literal one and the emphasis is on a word-for-word rendition of the original. The poetry has basically been turned into prose, though the rhymes of the last two lines hold slight traces of the poetic:

لاشيء يصلح للدفاع ضد منجل الزمن
سوى النسل الذي يتحداه حين يلبسك الكفن.

What is preserved is related to the content and the basic factual information. Such a procedure can be considered useful in the sense that it might help Arab students who have a poor understanding of English to understand the vocabulary items in a source language poem. In the translation we find, for instance,

(Line 1) count - أُعد, *tells the time –* تعلن الوقت

(Line 2)   brave day –النهار الشجاع, hideous night الليل المخيف

(Line 3)   behold - أرى, prime - النضج/ *violet - not translated but implied as* وردية *"rosy", past –* القديمة / = "old"

(Line 4)   sable - الأسود/, curls - المعقوص/ = "curled", silvered -فضض, o'er - بأكمله = "complete".

In spite of the translator's effort to provide an exact meaning for each word, however, he deviates either intentionally or because there was some misunderstanding of the source language text. For instance, we find *lofty trees* as الوفير الثمرات = 'trees abundant with fruits"; do I question as هل أسألك أن أستطيع/= "Can I, then, ask you..?" in which an affirmative statement is exchanged for an interrogative; and wastes of time as the verbal الذين يضيعون الوقت = "those who waste time."

In the translation there are three examples of creative innovation in:

a. *lofty trees* – الشجر الوفير الثمرات. It may be that in Arabic culture a lofty tree is one that provides us with fruit

b. *Time's scythe* – منجل الزمن which is a literal translation that maintains an expressive metaphor. Such a collocation is used in both languages and is effective even as a discrete item

c. *(Time/Death) takes thee hence* – حين يلبسك (الزمن/الموت) الكفن= "when time dresses you with a shroud".

Where the translator resorted to poetic devices familiar in Arabic there was a slight move towards the artistic but a lot was lost in this version of the poem. The translation as a whole is basically a paraphrase of the source poem in the target language. In his painstaking transfer of meaning at its lowest level (word-for-word) the translator distorted the syntax of the original so that in this version the use of non-poetic words lessened the poetic force. The translation fails to produce an artistic effect because the original music is muted and no alternative rhythm is put forward. Apart from the last two lines, there is no rhyme. The dramatic poetic effect was diminished because the translation renders the original imagery rather lifeless. The original poetic thoughts are provided but in a non-poetic manner. There is a shadow of the original feeling in this version but without the poetic force of the original diction. Although the translation of the last two lines lacks any rhythm known in Arabic poetry, we do sense a glimpse of the original feeling. All in all the diminution of the poetic devices of the original means that the translation is not an equal work of art in that they should work in an integral and collaborative manner to produce an effect.

8.5.2 *Creative Reformulation*

The following version of the poem by Ibrahim Za'rour represents a second method of translation. This version illustrates the translator's creative formulation of the source language poem.

إذ يمر الوقت محسوبا بدقات رتيبة ،

والنهار الباذخ الضوء هوى في وهدة الليل الرهيبة .
وأراها قد تولت – ذروة الإيناع في زهر البنفسج-
وتجاعيد سواد الشعر في فضة شيب تتوهج .
عندما تعرى من الأوراق أشجار ، ومن ثمر وفير ،
كان للقطعان ظلا ومراحا ... ويقيها من هجير .
حنطة الصيف استحالت حزما ... قش حصيد وقشور
حملتها عربات شائخات كالتوابيت إلى يوم النشور
هل من مجال بعد ذلك للسؤل عن الجمال ؟
والكل عاد في يباب الوقت محمول إلى نفس المآل :
حين الجمال وكل عذب مكره في هجر نفسه
إذ يرى الآخر ينمو ... يتوارى غب همسة .
لا شيء ينفع حين يشهر حد منجله الزمن
إلا التكاثر والتناسل حين يلبسك الكفن.
(إبراهيم زعرور)

[When time passes counted by monotonous beats
And day with its lavish light is sunk into the chasm of abominable night
And I can see has elapsed the violet's peak of mellowness
And the curls of black hair are glowing in silver grey
When the trees are barren of leaves and abundant fruit
That were for the herd's shade and rest and to protect them from the excessive
midday heat

The summer's wheat has become sheaves, harvest straw and dust
Carried by aged carts like coffins to the resurrection day,
Is it possible then to ask about beauty?
When everyone by this ravaging time is carried to the same destiny
When beauty as well as every sweet thing is forced to forsake it
When it sees another grow, disappear like a whisper,
Nothing will help when Time unsheathes the blade of its scythe
But to breed before you are dressed in shrouds.]
(Translated by Saad: 2002)

It is clear that when translating an English poem into Arabic it is difficult provide equivalent meter, rhythm and rhyme because of the phonetic and syntactic differences between the two languages. Za'rour's poem, however, shows the degree to which a translator can reproduce the form, rhythm, rhyme and other effects of the source language. Although he followed a line-by-line method of translation a great deal of the original is retained and Za'rour manages to provide a similar poetic effect through the employment of appropriate devices for carrying the poetic thoughts into the target language.

Among other things, Za'rour preserves the length, shape and the flow of the theme of the original. He follows the steps of the source language poem but at the same time maintains what is relevant to transferring the experience through the vehicle of another language. He uses similar devices very effectively ensuring that they are appropriate to Arabic. The structure of the rhyme in the source text is, for instance, a,b,a,b,c,d,c,d,e,f,e,f,g,g while that of the Za'rour's poem is a,a,b,b,c,c,c,c,d,d,e,e,f,f. This rhyming system ensures the enjoyment and coherence of the Arabic poem. Za'rour does not use the first person at the beginning but introduces وأراها = "I see" after the more neutral introduction of the first two lines:

إذ يمر الوقت محسوبا بدقات رتيبة،
والنهار الباذخ الضوء هوى في وهدة الليل الرهيبة.

[When time passes counted by monotonous beats
And the day with its lavish light is sunk into the chasm of abominable night.]

The Arabic poem follows Shakespeare's manner of depicting the theme of disintegration and, playing upon the theme of "sweets and beauties", reaches its peak in lines 11 and 12:

حين الجمال وكل عذب مكره في هجر نفسه
إذ يرى الآخر ينمو ...يتوارى غب همسة.

"When beauty as well as every sweet thing is forced to forsake it
When it sees the other grow, disappear like a whisper"

followed by the resolution of the last two lines

لا شيء ينفع حين يشهر حد منجله الزمن
إلا التكاثر والتناسل حين يلبسك الكفن
.

"Nothing will help when Time unsheathes the blade of its scythe
But to breed before you are dressed in shrouds."

The total picture of Za'rour's poem is evoked in diction (See 8.3.2.6) equal to the beauty and grandeur of the source text. For instance, دقات رتيبة، وهدة الليل، ذروة الإيناع،

يوم النشور، غب همسة Thus, this is not a lifeless literal translation of the type we saw in the first version above. The

Arabic poet has maintained the features we expect of a good poem providing an equivalent artistic experience. Obviously, different languages exhibit differences in detail with regard to words, collocations and the manner of presenting the imagery but Za'rour has produced a work of art true to the spirit of the source text. Though he treads in the footprints of his source Za'rour's poem has its own innovation and creativity.

8.5.3　Inspiration for a New Art Form

A third method of translation uses the source text as inspiration for creating a novel work. A new art form might be close to the original as we saw in Za'rour's version of Sonnet 12 *but an* extremely innovative piece of work might go far beyond the design and artistic experience of the source text. Accordingly, critics vary in their opinion of translations. For instance, Orientalists from Iran, Afghanistan, Britain and America *are unanimous in condemning Graves's Ruba'iyyat of Omar Khayaam as an unwarranted distortion of the poetry* (Bowen,1973:3). They consider it an abuse of Persian poetry. Despite the controversy, Graves's original edition was published and reprinted in the UK and the USA to be enjoyed by scores of readers.

Bowen (ibid:33) provides three variations on a theme and the following verse translations illustrate the way in which the same Khayyamic quatrain has been translated into English verse by Edward Fitzgerald (1879), Graves (1967) and Bowen (1973).

Fitzgerald IV,12
A Book of Verse underneath the Bough
A Jug of Wine, a Loaf of Bread – and Thou
Beside me singing in the Wilderness –
Oh. Wilderness were paradise enow!

Graves No.11
Should our day's portion be one mancel loaf
A haunch of mutton and a ground of wine
Set for us two alone on the wide plain,
No Sultan's bounty could evoke such joy.

Bowen No.12
If we were seated in a desert place,
Where I alone might gaze upon your face,
These simple victuals would our needs suffice:
A thigh of mutton in a dish of rice;
A loaf of bread of finest wheaten flour:
A flagon tall from which cool wine to pour..
There, in the day's long leisurely decline.
No Sultan's pleasures could compare with mine.

The theme is one of togetherness bringing joy to the writer. Each version uses different imagery and dramatic details and creates a different atmosphere to depict the same poetic situation. The deviation from the original can be sensed despite the fact that not all of the "translations" are based on the original Persian. Such differences as occur may create a view very different to that expressed in the original. For instance, Omar Khayyam's poem, which is meant by its writer to be mystical, has been erroneously accepted throughout the West as a drunkard's rambling profession of the hedonistic creed "let us eat and drink for tomorrow we die". (Graves & Shah, 1967:2)

The perception of the theme above by the three translators is one but the expressions vary. Wherever and whenever on earth we are, at whatever economic and social level, men and women read the theme in the same way or in ways so corresponding that they can adjust to a mutual recognition. When feelings of this kind are entailed there is a strong possibility of congruent rationality and Steiner (1975:373) explains that *the objectivity of the external world is invoked to validate a postulate of common understanding.*

The intricate details or the understanding of a remote language or alien culture are not important here. Content, or the development of the theme, is what provides an artistic experience. Steiner(1975: 375) enumerates various great works translated from exotic languages such as Fitzgerald's Rubaiyyat, Goethe's version of Hafiz and the like and comments that *some of the most persuasive translations in the history of the métier have been made by writers ignorant of the language from which they were translating* (ibid:375).

The degree of adequacy in translating a poem varies from translator to translator. If the second method outlined above in 6.5.2 with regard to Za'rour's poem is considered to be adequate, the third method exemplified by the three different translations just dealt with in regard to the Rubaiyyat demonstrates variation. A hermeneutic view explains this particular off-balance by suggesting that translators of this sort encircle and invade cognitively. We come home laden, thus again off-balance, having caused disequilibrium throughout the system by taking away from "the other" and by adding, though possibly with ambiguous consequence, to our own. (ibid:316).

Later on, Steiner (ibid: 316) says that *there is a dimension of loss and breakage. The source texts are dignified when translators deal with them. The act of transfer and paraphrase inflates the stature of the original and, ultimately, it becomes more prestigious.* We can feel a sense of superiority here and this is why Steiner asserts that there is a dimension of loss, breakage and imbalance. The translator, therefore, does a lot, he has padded, embroidered, "read into" – or too little – he has skimmed, elided, cut out awkward corners. There has been an outflow of energy from the source and an inflow into the receptor altering both and altering the harmonies of the whole system *(ibid:317)*. In this case the translator is not only a mirror that reflects an image but also a mirror which reflects light.

Steiner's attitude demeans the source text. The creativity of a good translator is apparent when appropriate devices that adequately convey the original experience are employed. Excessive interference will render some sort of experience but it will not be the intended experience. Changing the linguistic forms is legitimate, but to invade the source poet's experience is not.

As an independent entity, a work of art can survive across time if it has the potential to do so. We might practise some form of artistic skill which involves impinging on the existing art form in a foreign language but whatever we call it, it is not translation. We cannot presume that the foreign poet should have said something different from what he did say and that a translator's task is to produce the right text from what should have been said. A translator should reproduce the artistic experience as expressed by the poet at the time of writing the poem. The original experience speaks for itself. If the source text contains antique vocabulary and idioms that belong to a different era, a translator who sees something that is worth translating should be able to appreciate the text as it is and transfer the effect. Good translators submerge their sensibility and the genius of the target language in probing the artistic effect and in embodying this experience in the new language. When the experience is the aim, and translators yield to it, then, they alienate themselves from the linguistic source and, instead, they penetrate into the totality of the theme to achieve the transfer of stylised and codified markers.

8.6   Learning to Translate Poetry

In the previous section Shakespeare's Sonnet 12 was used to illustrate poetic structure and texture and the analysis showed how the use of the poetic devices of rhythm, rhyme, imagery, poetic through, feeling and diction brought coherence to Shakespeare's poem resulting in the production of an organic whole. A translator negotiating such a text must take care that excessive intervention does not demolish the totality of the original effect. Whatever a translator chooses to do, the main task is to maintain artistic coherence. The translator should keep, as much as possible, form and content intact. In the process of translation there may be some loss and some gain but the original artistic experience must be handled with care in order to provide artistic satisfaction in the target text which is similar to that of the source.

Three methods of translation were used to exemplify how poetry can be transferred from one language to another - literally, as a creative formulation, as inspiration for a something new. Whatever the case, the process of analysis and reconstruction involved is much more personal and makes a much greater demand on the translator's skill with both source and target language.

As was hinted at in 7.4, after practice with non-transactional prose, transition notes can be developed in such a way as to identify the dramatic development of a poem, complications of the theme and the denouement. As we saw with regard to The Daffodils, transition notes can be used first to establish a core, "uncoloured" meaning which can then be compared to the way in which the poem was actually expressed. The notes might lead to a relatively "unpoetic" translation of the poem in the early stages. More "poetic" notes illustrating, for instance, the poetic lexis can be used for translations moving beyond the basic as learners move along the path of perhaps eventually developing their own poem in the way illustrated in the by Za'rour's translation of Shakespeare.

At the beginning of the path leading to such skill, with regard to Sonnet 12, for instance, in which we saw the theme was one of deterioration leading towards death we might develop notes along the following lines from the early part of the poem.

"before"	"after"	Poetic imagery
Day	night	brave v hideous
a violet	faded	
black hair	grey	sable v silvered
lofty trees	bare	
green wheat	brown bundles	

After discussing the contrast between the description represented by the first two columns of the table and that represented by the third column, students might then be encouraged to explore similar "poetic" contrasts with regard to the violet, trees and wheat in order to complete the poetic imagery column. This type of exercise encourages the development of the facility to deal with appropriate poetic lexis.

An Arabic version of the notes might be something like:

الصورة الشعرية	"بعد"	"قبل"
شجاع مقابل قبيح	الليل	النهار
	ذابلة	زهرة
أسود مقابل فضي	أشيب	الشعر الأسود
	عارية	الأشجار
	حزم بنية	القمح الأخضر

This would lead to a depiction of the following set of contrasts

you die	*while*	*others grow*
	therefore	
breed	*and so*	*overcome death*

or in Arabic

ينمو الآخرون	بينما	تموت
ولذا		
تهزم الموت	وبذا	تناسل

Learners might use the transition notes to practise reconstruction in the source language both in oral and written form. Then, translation of the notes into Arabic will allow for attention to be paid to finding suitable equivalents so enabling learners to develop an understanding of poetic imagery and the skill of producing it. Discrete images can be developed within the framework of a textual totality to produce cohesive text. The practice of using various levels of expression from the more concrete to the more poetic for a range of different effects will enhance the learners' ability to

- cycle information in both languages
- cycle information at different levels for the purpose of developing skill with poetic imagery

Eventually, learners will be able to manipulate the language independently in order to be more creative themselves, a dimension that is essential in translating poetry. Work with transition notes will have helped them to discover features of poetic text (the value of poetic thought, feeling, diction, imagery, rhyme and rhythm) and will provide a level of control in their manipulation of these things. They can be used as the means for seeing the implications of the degrees of intervention available to the translator as they either keep to the basic plan of the source or move on to develop something quite novel. Working from notes rather than text allows for the production of cohesive text, whether prose or poetry, and is more likely to ensure that the result is not a literal, word-by-word rendering which ignores the poetic experience of the original.

Visual (3)

| | 2 |
| | |

| | 4 |
| | |

| | |
| 5 | |

| 6 | 7 |

Visual (4)

Visual (5)

Visual (6)

JOHN AND JACK

Visual (7)

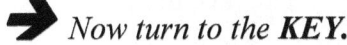 *Now turn to the KEY.*

8.7 Conclusion

When we compare transactional English and Arabic we see that each language fulfils the same set of communicative purposes integral to life in both English-speaking and Arabic-speaking contexts. Each has its own set of distinctive markers and discourse framework as the transmitter's intentions are transferred in a systematic way. Any translation from one language to the other does not require personal intervention on the part of the translator. Later, in the case study discussed in Chapter Three, we will see how the nature of the text imposes a consensus translation when transactional English text is translated into Arabic by a group of translators of relatively equal abilities.

A translator, who is in control of the core form of each communicative purpose, is able to move from a set of grammatical markers in one language to an appropriate set in another without the need for the replacement or rearrangement referred to above in 1.7 with regard to literary texts. Further, where necessary, a bilingual dictionary is likely to provide a straightforward equivalent for any vocabulary items that cannot be inferred from the overall context. (see 1.6)

Further, transactional language is frequently accompanied by non-visual support ranging from relatively representational photographs and drawings to relatively abstract graphs and charts. As indicated below in 4.6 and in the lesson material in the Appendix, this visual material has significance in the learning process.

Key

Try This (1): Language Variation (from page 16)

Table: Language Variation

		Text (a)	Text(b)	Text (c)
Mode	Written	✓	✓	✓
	Spoken	✓		
Subject Matter	Central		✓	✓
	Peripheral	✓		
Where	Report			✓
	Textbook			✓
	Novel	✓	✓	
	Social Gathering	✓		
Purpose	Educating			✓
	Setting a Scene		✓	
	Imparting Facts			✓
	Drawing Characters	✓		
	Stimulating the Imagination		✓	
	Socialising	✓		
Style	Personal	✓	✓	
	Impersonal			✓
	Subjective	✓	✓	
	Objective			✓
Syntax	Unpredictable	✓	✓	
	Predictable			✓
	Systematic			✓
	Fragmentary	✓	✓	
	Complete			✓
Lexis	Concrete			✓
	Abstract		✓	
	Idiomatic	✓		
Best Description	Social	✓		
	Factual			✓

			✓	
	Literary		✓	
Possible	Homogeneous			✓
Translation	Various	✓	✓	
	Individualistic	✓	✓	

Notes:

(i)   The topic of each text is roughly the same – the weather or atmospheric conditions. They each, however, deal with the topic very differently.

(ii)   Text (a) may be spoken and, as such, overheard at some social gathering. Alternatively it may be written and appear in a novel or short story. In either case the information about the weather is not the main purpose of the exchange. For the two speakers it provides an excuse for two strangers to chat. For the reader of a novel it provides information about the characters involved.

For instance, the use of *How do you do* as a greeting may indicate that the two people are meeting for the first time (as reinforced by the following *You from round here?* It can also be argued that they are older, perhaps middle class and probably meeting in a relatively formal situation. It may well be, however, that other English speakers reading this have had alternative experience of *How do you do?* In fact, a range of different interpretation is a central feature of social interchange. We choose a greeting, for instance, as being appropriate according to our individual assessment of the situation in which we meet people, our perceived relationship to them, their age, their apparent social status and the like. We make such decisions according to a bundle of almost indescribable clues dependent on our experience and cultural awareness. Such language is extremely personal and individualistic in nature.

This is reflected in the syntax which is often fragmentary - *You from round here?* As opposed to the "normal" form *Are you from around here?* Or *Not bad really. Could be worse.* for *The weather is not bad really. It could be worse.* Similarly idiomatic vocabulary is typical of such social language. For instance, the use of *find* in *How are you finding it?* = "Do you like it" is a long way from the central meaning of "locating" or "coming upon".

(iii) Text (b) is another example of literary language of the type discussed above in1.6as such it is highly personal and individualistic. It stimulates the imagination as it sets the scene for what is to follow. Some readers may feel a sense of unease, others one of fear, others one of eeriness, others one of anticipation and so on. Text (c) is a further example of transactional language of the type illustrated in 1.4. It is impersonal and predictable as it uses facts about weather either to educate the reader in the manner of a text book or perhaps to provide factual information about the weather in a report on the progress of filming.

Try This (2): Communicative Purposes (from page 34)

Text (d): Narration

Vernon / arrived / home / from work (SVAA) and made / a cup of coffee (SVO). He / poured out / a mugful (SVO) and sat down / to enjoy it (SVA). He / took / a sip (SVO). He / smiled (SV) and began to relax (SV) and the various trials of the day / receded (SV).

> The underlined verbs are in the **stem+*ed*** form and are **dynamic** in that each refers to an action that has been carried out. The discourse is organised **sequentially** outlining 7 steps in the order in which they occurred.

Text (e): Description of a Man-Controlled Process

The soil / is prepared (SV) and / holes / are made / at fixed intervals (SVA). Fertiliser / is put / into the holes (SVA) and / coffee seedlings / are planted / four to a hole (SVA). During the growing period / they are / carefully / tended (SV). When the coffee berries are mature / they / are picked / by hand (SVA).

> The underlined verbs are **passive** in form (i.e. [stem/stem+*s*] + [stem+*ed*]) and are **dynamic** in that each refers to a step in the description of a process controlled by man. The discourse is thus organised **sequentially** to show the steps in the process.

Text (f): Instruction

Measure / the coffee / into a warmed jug (VOA). Add / the correct amount of boiling water (VO) and stir / it / well (VOA). Leave / it / for a minute (VOA) and draw / the edge of a spoon /

*across the top (*VOA*). Stand / the pot / in a warm place / for four minutes (*VOAA*). Strain / it (*VO*) and serve / it (*VO*).*

The underlined verbs are **stem** in form and are **dynamic** in that each refers to a step to be carried out. The discourse is organise **sequentially** to indicate the order in which the steps are to be carried out

Text (g): Description of a Natural Process or Cycle

*The coffee plant / produces / white flowers (*SVO*). Soon / the stigma / receives / pollen / from the anthers (*SVOA*) and fertilisation / occurs (*SV*). Seeds / develop (*SV*) and ripen (*SV*). Some seeds / find / soil in which to grow (*SVO*) and under suitable conditions / a root / bursts through / the seed case (*ASVO and then / a shoot / develops (*SV*).*

The underlined verbs are either **stem+s** like *produces, receives* or **stem** like *develop, ripen*. They are **dynamic** in that each refers to a step in a process that occurs naturally. They are arranged sequentially as they describe how the cycle of growth occurs.

Text (h): Stative Description

*There / are / many different types of coffee (*thereVC*). They / have / different flavours (*SVO*). The coffees of Africa / have / a strong flavour (*SVO*). They / are / often / very bitter (*SVAC*). Blue mountain coffee / comes / from Jamaica (*SVC*). It / is / a mixture of coffees (*SVC*) and has / an unusual taste (*SVO*). There / is / a wide range of Brazilian coffee (*thereVC*. It / is / not / all good (*SVAC*) but it / has / a harsher taste than other coffees (*SVO*). Colombian coffee / is / strong and rich with a slightly bitter taste (*SVC*).*

The underlined verbs are either **stem** like *are, have* or **stem+s** like *is, has, comes*. They are stative in that they do not refer to an action of any kind. The discourse is organised according to concept, beginning with a generalisation about coffee and then going on to detail the origin and flavour of different coffees.

Text (i): Narration
The Chieftain / <u>led</u> / his charges / through the door of the Keep (SVOA). Then / they / <u>caught sight of</u> / the poet (SVO). Sarah / <u>rushed</u> / to him (SVA) and <u>slipped</u> / a hand / inside his shirt / to feel the beat of his heart (SVOAA). She / <u>raised</u> / a cup / to his lips (SVA).

   This text has the same features as Text (d) above –

stem+ed, *dynamic verbs arranged* **sequentially** *in order*

to outline a series of events in the order that they

happened.

Try This (3): Non-Verbal Information (from page 37)

Visual (2): A single representational drawing of this type is most often used to communicate descriptive information of the stative type. A possible verbal match would be a "word picture" something like:

> *Bedford is a small village. It is bounded on here sides by fields and a river cuts across the north east. A stone church dominates the village. It has a square tower. There are several houses grouped around the church They are each set in a small field.*

Visual (3): This sequenced visual communicates a set of instructions. Each numbered step is an abstraction of an action to be carried out. This is indicated by the use of arrows, disembodied thread and scissors. At the very simplest level we can understand a step for each diagram:

> *Take some sheets of paper. Fold them in half. Make some holes down the fold. Use the holes to sew the sheets together. Tie the thread firmly. Fold the pages over and trim the edges.*

Visual (4):   A series of arrows imposed on a stylised drawing of this kind is used conventionally to indicate some type of natural process or cycle. In this case the arrows are imposed on a stylised rendition of large entities in nature – the tree symbolising vegetation in general, the deer symbolising animals and so on. This visual provides information about the water cycle which could be expressed in simple terms as:

> *Rain falls on the earth. It runs into streams and rivers. From here it goes to lakes or oceans or it is taken up by animals and plants. Moisture evaporates from the surface of the water and animals and plants transpire. This forms clouds and eventually rain falls to the earth again.*

Visual (5)   This sequence of diagrams indicates steps in a man-controlled process. It differs from Visual (3) in that the abstractions provided are "larger than life" – a rubber tree symbolises a plantation and is outside the normal person's everyday experience. (In contrast the sheets of paper, thread, needle, scissors and the like of Visual (3) are everyday objects well within the day-to-day environment of most of us.) At the simplest level Visual (5) communicates information about the process of producing rubber in an essentially non-mechanised manner:

> *Rubber trees are tapped. The latex is poured into a bucket. It is mixed with acid in a vat. Rubber sheets are produced by rollers and dried in the sun. The sheets are baled and weighed. Finally they are transported by road, rail and sea.*

Visual (6)   This sequence of pictures shows easily recognisable characters within a clearly seen background. The sequence moves through to tell the story of John and Jack's camping expedition:

> *John and Jack crawled out of their tent and went canoeing. After that they took water from the river back to heir camp. They washed their cups and plates and gathered their belongings together … …*

Visual (7)   This visual shows single pictures linked, not by a sequence of occurrence, but by topic, that of bridges. This indicates stative description but, unlike that of the village of Bedford, indicates a comparative or classificatory purpose with regard to the description – possibly something like:

> *Bridges differ according to their construction and purpose. Some bridges are very simple. For instance, in some the supports are piles of stone. Flat stone slabs are placed on these to provide the deck. Such bridges are foot bridges.*
>
> *Other bridges are for carrying roads and railways. These are more complex. Some road bridges are made of brick. They are arched to carry heavy loads. There may be a*

single arch over a narrow river. Wide rivers are spanned by ....

Try This (4) **Transition Notes: Instruction** (from page 65)

1. The 10 steps are:

    1. Warm
    2. Measure
    3. Boil
    4. Add
    5. Stir
    6. Leave
    7. Draw
    8. Leave
    9. Strain
    10. Serve

Notes:

(i)   The first paragraph does not include steps in the sequence of instructions. Rather, it provides advice of the type referred to in 2.2.1.

(ii)   *Measure the coffee into a warmed jug* is a relatively sophisticated way of referring to the two steps: 1 *Warm a jug* and 2 *Measure some water into it*. This is also true of *Add the correct amount of boiling water –* 3 *Boil some water* and 4 *Add it to the coffee*. The assumption is that an important aspect of the comprehension of the two sentences involved is the ability to retrieve the "core" or basic steps from the more sophisticated expression in the original text.

Similarly, *some water* is a core version of *the correct amount of water* (see 4.3 for further discussion)

2. Possible "core" transition notes are:

11. Warm	*a jug*	
2. Measure	*some coffee*	*into the jug*
3. Boil	*some water*	
4. Add	*it*	*(to the coffee)*
5. Stir	*it*	
6. Leave	*it*	
	for 1 minute	
7. Draw	*a spoon*	*across the top*
8. Leave	*the pot*	
	for 4 minutes	
9. Strain	*the coffee*	
10. Serve	*it*	

3. The system of reference can be shown thus:

1. Warm	*a jug*	
2. Measure	*some coffee*	*into the jug*
3. Boil	*some water*	
4. Add	*it*	*(to the coffee)*
5. Stir	*it*	
6. Leave	*it*	
	for 1 minute	
7. Draw	*a spoon*	*across the top*
8. Leave	*the pot*	
	for 4 minutes	
9. Strain	*the coffee*	
10. Serve	*it*	

We note that for:

- "first mention" of a "countable noun" *a*+N is used – *a jug*

- "first mention" of an "uncountable noun" *some*+N is used – *some coffee,*

  some water
- "back reference" *the*+N is used with both countable and uncountable nouns – *the jug, the coffee, the top [of the coffee], the pot*
- *it* is used to refer back to nouns immediately mentioned for variation

4.   A simple core reconstruction of the information might be something like:

> *Warm a jug. Measure some coffee into the jug. Boil some water. Add it to the coffee. Stir it. Leave it for a minute. Draw a spoon across the top. Leave it for 4 minutes. Strain the coffee and serve it.*

We note that each sentence component contains only one idea, the type of language McEldowney defines as core (4.3)

5.   A possible set of core notes would be:

1. Hammer	*two nails*	*through some wood*
2. Turn	*the wood*	*over*
3. Take	*two candles*	
4. Push	*a candle*	*on each nail*
5. Place	*a watch*	*near the candles*
6. Light	*one candle*	

7. Wait			for 5
minutes			
8. Paint	a line	on the other candle	
9. Repeat	this procedure		every
5 minutes			

Try This (5): **Transition Notes: Narration** (from page 67)

1.   Transition notes of the narrative sequence might look something like:

1. Vernon	arrived		home
2. He	made	some coffee	
3.	poured out	a mugful	
4.	sat down		
5.	took	a sip	
6.	smiled		
7.	relaxed		
8. The day	receded		from	his

mind

(iv)   We note the same system of reference with regard to *a*+N, *some*+N and *the*+N as seen in the instruction texts occurs here. There is also back reference to *Vernon* with the pronoun *he* and back reference with *his* when his mind is referred to.

(v)   A core reconstruction of the information from the notes might be:

> *Vernon arrived home. He made some coffee. He poured out a mugful. He sat down and took a sip. He smiled and relaxed. The day receded from his mind.*

(vi)   A descriptive column could be added to the notes thus:

1. Vernon	arrived		home
[tense]			
2. He	made	some coffee	
3.	poured out	a mugful	
4.	sat down		
5.	took	a sip	
[strong/bitter]			
6.	smiled		
7.	relaxed		
8. The day	receded		from his mind

(vii)   Description could be added to the core narrative reconstruction thus:

> *Vernon arrived home. He was tense He made some coffee. He poured out a mugful. He sat down and took a sip. It was strong and bitter. He smiled and relaxed. The day receded from his mind.*

2.   Possible notes for the narrative of Bonnet's experiment together with descriptive

comment might be:

French

a biologist

in insects & communication

- -
- - - - - - - - - - - - -

1. (B)	placed	a flower	on	a	table
[large/swarming with ants]					
2.	put	some sugar	at the other end		
3.(The As)	moved		backwards & forwards		
4. (B)	drew	his finger	across the trail		
5.(The As)	moved		sideways		
6.(Some As)	recognised	some other ants			
7.(The As)	reconnected	their trail			

- -- - -
- - - - - - - - - - - - - -

a scent trail

*Try This (6):*Transition Notes: Stative Description

(from page 69)

   1. (i)   2 parts: the motte & the bailey

     (ii)   *a hill, small, circular, a ditch around it, a tower on top*

     (iii)

"Appearance"

The Motte	*The Bailey*
a hill	a field
Small	Larger
Circular	Circular
X	to the south

"Defences"

The Motte		The Bailey	
a ditch	Around the motte	a ditch	around the bailey
		a bank	inside the ditch
		a stockade	on the bank

(v)

"Buildings"

the motte		the bailey			
a tower	on the top	some soldiers' quarters	square	in the middle	
		a chapel	square	in the north	
		some stables	rectangular		
		some storehouses			

(vi)

"Keswick Castle"

	the motte		the bailey			
appearance	a hill		a field			
	Small		Larger			
	Circular		Circular			
			to the south			
defences	a ditch	around the motte	a ditch		around the bailey	
			a bank		inside the ditch	
			a stockade		on the bank	
buildings	a tower	in the top	some soldiers' quarters	square	in the middle	
			a chapel	square	in the north	
			some stables	rectangular		
			some storehouses			

(vii)   A simple reconstruction would treat each part of the castle separately, something like:

The motte is a hill. It is small. It is circular. There is a ditch around it and a tower on the top.

The bailey is a field. It is larger than the motte. It is circular. It is to the south. There is a ditch around the bailey, a bank inside the ditch and a stockade on the bank. There are several buildings in the bailey. There are some soldiers' quarters, a chapel, some tables and some storehouses. The soldiers' quarters are square and are in the middle. The chapel is also square. It is to the north. The stables are rectangular.

2.   **"Coffees"**

Country	*taste*	*example*
Africa	strong/unusual	
Jamaica	unusual	
Brazil	harsher	Blue Mountain
Colombia	strong/rich/bitter	

Try This (7): **Transition Notes: Mixed Communicative Purposes** (from page 71)

***Text (p):*Communicative Purpose:** Description of a Man-Controlled Purpose.

"Lumbering"

1. Preparing	(Ps)	are made in summer	(Ts)	are selected	
			(Cs)	are prepared	
			(Rs)	are built	
2. Felling	(Ts)	are felled in winter	(Ts)	are felled	
			(Bs)	are cut off	
3. Transporting the snow	(T)	is transported	(Ls)	are dragged	over
ice				are piled	on the
the rivers	in spring			are floated	down
. [Milling	(T)	is processed]	(Ls)	are sorted	
				are fed	into
mills					
				are cut	into
planks					

An overall sequence of the main steps might form the first paragraph:

> *Preparations are made in summer. Trees are felled in winter. Timber is transported to the mills in spring. [It is processed at the mill.]*

Details of each main part of the process might be expressed thus:

> *In summer trees are selected. Campsites are prepared and roads are built. Trees are felled in winter and the branches are cut off. The logs are dragged over the snow and they are piled on the ice. In the spring the logs are floated down the rivers. They are sorted and fed into mills. They are then cut into planks.*

Text (q): **Communicative Purpose:** Description of a Natural Process

"The Water Cycle"

	The Normal Cycle		The Caspian Cycle
Moisture	1. falls	on the land	1.
	2. flows	into rivers	2. enters
4. flows	3. goes	to the sea	3.
	5. fills		
	4. evaporates	from the surface	6.
evaporates			
	5. falls	on the land	7. falls

Note:

(i)   The Caspian cycle has two extra steps – seven rather than the "normal" five. This is indicated on the notes above by the two extra steps, *flows* and *fills* to the right of the two steps said to be held in common by the two cycles.

(ii) The step *enters* in the Caspian cycle is a summary of the three steps *falls, flows, goes* which have already been enumerated for the route of moisture going to an ocean – this, *Water enters the Caspian in the normal way.*

A modification of the table above indicating the cyclic nature of the information and the overlap of the two cycles might be something like:

falls

evaporates   flows

goes

flows

fills

A core reconstruction might be something like:

> In the normal cycle water falls on the land. It flows into rivers. It goes to the sea. It evaporates from the surface. It falls on the land.

> In the Caspian cycle water falls on the land. It flows into three rivers. It goes to the Caspian. It flows into the desert. It fills the Kara Gulf> It evaporates from the surface. It falls on the land again.

A more sophisticated output might compare the two thus:

> In both the normal and Caspian cycles moisture falls on the land, flows into rivers and goes to the sea. In the normal cycle it then evaporates from the surface and falls on the land again. Before these steps in the Caspian cycle, however, water flows into the desert from the Caspian sea and fills the Kara Gulf. It then evaporates from the surface and falls on the land again.

Text (r): **Communicative Purpose:** A Stative Description

"Corridors"

Corridors	Orientation	Length	Dimensions			Position	
1	N-S	427´	(F) 16´x 8´ (C) 4´				
2-7	E-W		Smaller	straight	open	off C1	at regular intervals
8			Smaller	curved	closed		

"Rooms"

Rooms	Position		Size	Shape	Purpose
1-3	½-way along C1	side-by-side on the east	Small	rectangular	for bathing
4		opens from C1	24´ square	square	for fortune telling
5	at the end of C1	to the W of R4	24´ square	square	for consulting
6		to the E of R4	30´ square	square	
7		to the N or R6	Smaller		
8		to the S of R6	Smaller		

A core reconstruction would be something like:

> *The caves contain seven corridors. One goes north-south. It is 427 feet long. The walls are 16 feet high. The floor is eight feet wide and the ceiling is four feet wide. It is straight.*
>
> *Six other corridors go east-west. They are smaller. They are on the west. Six are straight and open. The seventh is curved and closed.*
>
> *There are three room half-way along the first corridor. They are on the east. They are side-by-side. They are small and rectangular. They were for bathing.*
> *There are five more rooms at the end of the first corridor. One opens from the corridor. It is twenty-four feet square. It was for fortune telling There is another room west of this room. It is also twenty-four feet square. It was for consulting. There is another room to the east. It is thirty-feet square. There is one room to the north of this room and another to the south. They are smaller.*

A more sophisticated version from the same transition notes might be:

> *The caves at Cumae consist of rooms and corridors. The main corridor runs north-south and seven smaller ones run east-west. The north-south corridor is 427 feet long, the walls are 16 feet high, the floor is 8 feet wide and the ceiling if 4 feet wide. It is straight. Six of the east-west corridors are also straight and they are open to the sea while the other east—west corridor is curved and closed to the sea.*
>
> *There are three small rectangular rooms on the east of the main corridor. They were for bathing. There are six larger rooms at the end of the main corridor. The one opening from the corridor is twenty-four feet square and*

was for fortune telling. There is another room to the east of this and one to the west. The one on the west is also twenty-four feet square and was for hearing fortunes. The room to the east is thirty feet square. It has a smaller room on the north and another room to the south.

Text (s): **Communicative Purpose:** A Man-Controlled Purpose

"Early Houses"

| A hole | was dug | |
| [rectangular] | | |

Supports	were constructed	
[stones]		
A pole	was fixed	at each end
[forked]		
A ridge pole	was laid	across them
Other poles	were cut	to the same length [for rafters]
The rafters	were leaned	along each side
Branches	were laid	across the rafters
Turf	was cut	from grassland
[square]		
	were laid	over the branches

Note:

As is common in sequenced language, there are, in the text, two examples of *had* marking out of sequence (*had been cut*). The cutting of the poles took place before they were leaned along the house and the cutting of the turf took place before it was placed on the roof. In the core notes and simple reconstruction these steps are related in the order they were carried out.

A simple reconstruction would consist of only the steps in the process while a more sophisticated version would include the stative description shown in the square brackets:

> *A hole was dug. [It was rectangular.] Supports were constructed. [They were stone.] A pole was fixed at each end. [They were forked]. A ridge pole was laid across them. Other poles were cut to the same length. [They were for rafters]. The rafters were leaned along each side. Branches were laid across the rafters. Turf was cut from grassland. [The pieces were square]. They were laid over the branches.*

Try This (8): **Colouring a Scene** (from page 124)

1.   McEldowney (1992:60) produces a possible **dreary** description:

> *It was a **dreary** early evening and the **grey** of the grass was a **dull sodden** colour. The **bleak** light came through the **leaden** beech leaves and the cedar showed the lines of its **drabness** against a **dull drizzle-laden** sky*

Here *dreary* is "defined" by the adjectives *dull, sodden, bleak, leaden, dull, drizzle-laden* reinforced by the associated nouns *grey* and *drabness*. Though the same frame has been used this is a long way from the *beautiful* description of the original from Christie.

Similarly, with a change of colour she turns the following into a **frightening** description:

It was a **frightening** early evening and the **well** of the grass was a **dark intimidating cavern**. **Violent flashes of lightening** came through the **starkness** of the beech leaves and the cedar showed the lines of a **demon** against the **turbulent flash-riven** sky.

Your descriptions are probably quite different to those above and will be based on your own experience of the different phenomena involved.

2. (i)   A possible Arabic translation of the uncoloured description is:

(ii) A *dreary* description might be:

(iii)   A *creepy* description might be:

Try This (9): **Changing Characters** (from page 130)

1. (i)   A possible English first paragraph from the grandmother notes might be:

> *The grandmother walked into the room and sat on her chair. She picked up her glasses and looked out across the yard.*

(ii)   Possible notes for paragraphs 2 and 3 might be:

An intervening space defined by boundaries

The Yard

What	*where*
a wall	on either side
some weeds	in the cracks
some waste land	beyond the yard

An active scene beyond no-mans-land

The Waste Land

Who	*Activity*	*where*
some dogs	running barking Darting	around the wasteland at each other
some children	chasing each other screaming Laughing	around some bushes
some scraps of paper	blowing around	

Obviously your notes will be different but check them to see that they follow the appropriate pattern.

(iii)A possible grandmother story from the notes above would be:

> *The grandmother walked into the room and sat on her chair. She picked up her glasses and looked out across the yard.*
>
> *The yard had a wall on each side and there were some weeds growing in the cracks. There was some waste land at the end of the garden.*
>
> *Beyond the yard some dogs were running around the wasteland, barking and darting at each other. Some children were chasing each other around some bushes, screaming and laughing. Some scraps of paper were blowing around.*

2. Complete burglar notes might be:

> *The Burglar*
> came
> opened
> went
> looked

> *An intervening space defined by boundaries*
> **The Passage Way**

what	*where*
the walls	on each side
some paintings	on the walls
a mirror	on the right
a dining room	beyond the passage way

An active scene beyond no-mans-land
The Dining Room

Who	*Activity*	*where*
men & women	sitting clattering their knives & forks clinking their glasses	at a table
a girl	Singing	
a man	accompanying her	at a piano

A passage about a burglar in English might be:

> *A burglar came through some bushes, opened a window and went into the room. He looked down a passage way.*
>
> *There were paintings on the walls on each side and there was a mirror on the right. There was a dining room at the end of the passage way.*
>
> *Beyond the passage way men and women were sitting around a table in the dining room, clattering their knives and forks and clinking their glasses. A girl was singing and a man was accompanying her at the piano.*

3. Possible coloured words for the two characters might be:

The Grandmother

walked	سارت	**doddered**	تقدم
بوهن			
sat		**lowered**	
picked up		**fumbled for**	
looked		**peered**	

The Burglar

came	قدم	crawled	زحف
opened		slid	
went		crept	
looked		peeped	

though obviously yours will be rather different. Look at your coloured words, however, and make sure they are consistent so that you are able to say what sort of person our character is.

Appendix

The English lesson materials included here are two examples of those worked out in detail by McEldowney and used by her in the classroom and in teacher training sessions. The purpose of the materials is to lead students first to extract the essential information from textual material and then to be able to speak and write their own versions of that same information. There are cycles of increasing sophistication involved. It is argued that trainee translators can follow this pattern first to improve their own English skills and then, as illustrated by the Arabic tasks, begin on the path to developing their translation skills. The tasks illustrated can be either teacher-led or pupil-led.

A.1   A Learning Methodology for Sequenced Language

Tortoises

1   *The normal habitat for a tortoise is dry, sandy ground. They do not like the damp.*

2   *In captivity they need a compound about 10 feet by 4 feet in a sunny, sheltered place. The compound should be fenced by a frame of wooden posts about 1 foot high covered with wire netting. Dig out the soil inside the compound to about 9 inches. Replace it with sand and scatter some stones on the top.*

3   *There needs to be a shelter in the compound. It can be made of a wooden box about 7 inches high, 2½ feet wide and 2 feet broad with an entrance hole about 8 inches wide. Place the shelter in one corner of the compound, standing on four bricks.*

4   Sink a plastic container in the ground so that it is at ground level and fill it with water. It should be about 2 feet by one foot.

5   Tortoises hibernate from October to April. For hibernation put the tortoise in a wooden box and pack some hay around it. Now store the box in a dry, cool place like a cellar. In the following April place the box on its side in the compound and put some fresh hay in the shelter. The tortoise will come out when it wakes up and begin eating again.

1.   Read *Tortoises* quickly. Find the paragraph for each of the following. Write the paragraph number in the brackets.

providing some water ( )

making a shelter ( )

providing for hibernation ( )

making a compound ( )

- -

- - - - - - - - - - - -

Key (1):   some water (4); a shelter (3); hibernation (5); the compound (1)

- -

- - - - - - - - - - - -

2.   Put the following steps in the correct order to make a tortoise compound:

Scatter   Place   Dig out

Stand

Replace   Fill   Sink

Key (2):   1 Dig out; 2 Replace; 3 Scatter; 4 Place; 5 Stand; 6 Sink; 7 Fill

3.   Complete the following:

	1	**Make**	**a compound**
To do this,	1.1	Make	
	1.2	Dig out	
	1.3	Replace	
	1.4	Scatter	
	2	**Make**	**a shelter**
	2.1	Place	
	2.2	Stand	
	3	**Make**	**a drinking bowl**
To do this,	3.1	Sink	
	3.2	Fill	

Key (3):

	1	**Make**	**a compound**	
To do this,	1.1	Make	a fence	
	1.2	Dig out	the soil	to

about 9 ins.

	1.3	Replace	it	with
some sand				
	1.4	Scatter	some stones	on
the sand				
	2	**Make**	**a shelter**	
	2.1	Place	four bricks	in a
corner				
	2.2	Stand	the shelter	on
them				
	3	**Make**	**a drinking bowl**	
To do this,	3.1	Sink	a container	in the
ground				
	3.2	Fill	it	with
		water		

- - -- -

4.   Now speak the instructions and then write them.

- -

Key (4):   Learners should be "drilled" in speaking instructions from the transition notes modelled on:

> *Make a compound. To do this, make a fence. Dig out the soil to about 9 ins. Replace it with some sand. Scatter some stones on the sand.*
>
> *Make a shelter. Place four bricks in a corner. Stand the shelter on them.*

Make a drinking bowl. To do this, sink a container in the ground and fill it with water.

As they become familiar with the instructions they should be encouraged to add naturally some of the features of natural speech – *First you make a compound. Then...*

Once they are fluent they should then write the instructions but in the written form illustrated in the model above.

----

5.   Translate your transition notes from 3 into Arabic. To do this, begin with column 1, then complete column 2 and then column 3.

Key (5):

Learners should be expected to produce Arabic transition notes. They should be encouraged to build them up column by column - discussing verb marking as compared to English; the 2 reference systems with regard to pronouns, determiners, case; the nature of the sentence types in both systems.

----

6.   Speak the instructions in Arabic and then write them.

----

7.   Read the text *Tortoises* again and complete the following table:

A Tortoise Compound

	Parts	*Dimensions*	*Materials*
The Compound	/////		/////
(i) The Fence	(a)		
	(b)	/////	
(ii) The Shelter	(a)		
	(b)		/////
(iii) The Bowl			

- -

- - - - - - - - - - - - -

Key (6):

	Parts	*Dimensions*	*Materials*
The	/////	10ft x 4 ft	/////

- 263 -

Compound			
(i) The Fence	(a) a frame	1 ft high	wooden
	(b) some netting		wire
(ii) The Shelter	(a) a box	7ins x 2½ft x 2ft	wooden
	(b) an entrance	8ins wide	
(iii) The Bowl	a container	2ft x 1ft	plastic

----

8.   Look at the diagram below. On it, label:

the shelter, the drinking bowl, a wooden post,

some netting, a tortoise

and mark the dimensions where indicated.

Key (7):

the drinking bowl   the

shelter

a tortoise

a wooden post   some netting

----

9.   Add the information from the table to your instructions.

Begin like this:

> *Make a compound 10 feet by 4 feet. To do this*
> *make a fence with a wooden frame and wire*
> *netting cover. It should be 1 foot high. Dig out*
> *... .....*

Key (8):   The more detailed instructions might be something

like:

> *Make a compound 10 feet by 4 feet. To do*
> *this make a fence with a wooden frame and wire*
> *netting cover. Dig out the soil in the compound to*
> *about 9 inches. Replace it with some sand. Scatter*
> *some stones on the sand.*
> *Make a shelter from a wooden box. It*
> *should be 7 inches by 2½ feet by 2 feet. The*
> *entrance should be 8 inches wide. Place four*
> *bricks in a corner of the compound and place the*
> *shelter on them.*
> *Make a drinking bowl from a plastic*
> *container. It should be 2 feet by 1 foot. Sink it into*
> *the ground and fill it with water.*

----

9.   Look at the table you made in 7 above. Now make an Arabic table of the same information.

Look at the diagram in 8 above and write suitable Arabic labels under the English ones.

- -

- - - - - - - -

11.   (i)   Now look at paragraph 5 in the Tortoise Text on page 1.Make

transition notes about the steps to be carried out for hibernation.

(ii)   Translate your transition notes into English.

(iii)   Use your transition notes to write about hibernation in Arabic.

- -

- - - - - - - -

Key 9: Possible English transition notes might be:

In October	put	the tortoise	in a box	
	Pack	some hay	around it	
	Store	the box	in the cellar	
In April	Place	the box	on its side	in the compound
	Put	some hay	in the shelter	

A.2   A Learning Methodology for Non-Sequenced Language

Castra

The plan shows a reconstruction of Castra, a Roman town in Britain, octagonal in shape. The town is protected by a high wall with a surrounding ditch. Further protection was afforded by the fact that the wall is broken by only four gates - in the north, east, south and west. These were easy to protect against invaders and would have been closed and barred at night. The area inside the walls is divided into seventeen regular sections by a series of straight roads.

In the middle is the forum in which were held public meetings. It consists of four separate buildings arranged in a square around an open space. The basilica or law court, a long rectangular building on the plan, forms the west side of the square.

There are four religious buildings on the plan – a Christian church and three temples. The church is close to the forum, just to the south-east of the central section. It is easy to identify because of its cruciform shape. Two of the temples are by the east gate – one close to the wall and the other in the section next to the church while the third is directly to the south of the basilica. It is a tall circular building with supporting pillars and a domed roof while the other two temples are rectangular, two-storied buildings.

Another two important buildings in the town are the C-shaped inn close to the south gate and the baths in a triangular section close to the inn. The amphitheatre, where games were held, is outside the town wall.

1.   Read the first paragraph about Castra and complete the following table:

Castra

Where	Shape	Protection		Layout	
		What	Where	What	Appearance
				/////////	/////////

- -

- - - - - - - - - - - -

Key (1):

Castra

Where	Shape	Protection		Layout	
		What	Where	What	Appearance
in Roman Britain	octagonal	a wall	around the town	several roads	straight
		a ditch	surrounding the wall	17 sections	regular
		4 gates	in the N, E, S & W	/////////	/////////

- -

- - - - - - - - - -

2.   Use your table to speak about Castra.

- -

- - - - - - - - - -

Key (2):   An appropriate early model might be something like:

> *Castra was a town in Roman Britain. It was octagonal in shape. It was protected by a wall around the town, a ditch*

surrounding the wall and four gates, one in the north, one in the east, one in the south and one in the west. There were several straight roads in the town. They divided the town into 17 regular sections.

--------- -

3. Now read the rest of the information about Castra and complete the following table:

Places of Interest

	Landmark	Parts	Where	Appearance		Purpose
1						
2						
3						
4						
5						
6						
7						
8						
9						

-------------- -

Key (3):

Places of Interest

	Landmark	Parts	Where	Appearance	Purpose
1	the forum	4 buildings a central space	in the middle	square	for public meetings
2	The basilica		in the forum	rectangular	for a law court

- 269 -

			along the W			
3	a church		near the forum	cruciform		for Christians
			SE of the middle section			
4	a temple		by the E gate	rectangular	2-storied	
			near the wall			
5	a temple		by the E gate	rectangular	2-storied	
			near the church			
6	a temple		S of the basilica	circular, tall	with pillars & a domed roof	
7	an inn		near the S gate	C-shaped		
8	some baths		close to the inn			
			in a triangular section			
9	an amphitheatre		outside the walls			for games

- -

- - - - - - - - - - - -

4.   Use your table to speak about the places of interest in Castra. Begin *On the plan of Castra the forum consists of* .....

- -

- - - - - - - - - - - -

Key (4):   A possible model would be something like:

On the plan of Castra the forum consists of four buildings around a central space. It is in the middle. It is square and was used for public meetings.

The basilica is in the forum, along the west. It is rectangular and was used for a law court.

The church is near the church, SE of the middle section. It is cruciform and was used for Christians.

The first temple is by the E gate, near the wall. It is rectangular and two-storied.

The second temple is by the East gate, near the church. It is rectangular and two-storied.

The third temple is south of the basilica. It is circular and tall with pillars and a domed roof.

The baths are close to the inn in a triangular section.

The amphitheatre is outside the walls and was used for games.

5.   Now look at the plan of Castra below and complete the Key. To do this, write the numbers 1 to 10 from the plan in the appropriate places on the Key below:

	the basilica
	the baths
	the church
	the amphitheatre
	the inn
	the forum
	the first temple
	the second temple

	the third temple
	X

- -

- - - - - - - - - -

Key (5):

5	the basilica
7	the baths
3	the church
10	the amphitheatre
1	the inn
4	the forum
9	the first temple
8	the second temple
2	the third temple
6	X

- -

- - - - - -

6.   Look at the two tables you completed in 1 & 3 and above
and write about Castra. The first paragraph should be about
Castra in general and the second about the places of interest.

- -

- - - - - -- -

Key (6):   These two paragraphs should parallel the spoken practice modelled above with regard to the two tables.

- - - - - - - -

8.   Look at your two Arabic tables and write about Castra in Arabic. Write a paragraph from each table.

- - - - - - -

Bibliography

References

Baker, M. (1992)   *In Other Words*, Routledge,
London & New York

Bassnet, S. (1980)   *Translation Studies*, Methuen,
London

Beaugrande, R. (1978)   *Factors in a Theory of Poetic
Translating*, Van
                Gorcum, Assen, The Netherlands

Beaugrande, R. (1980)   *Text, Discourse and Process*,
Longman, London

Beaugrande, R. & Dressler, W. (1981) *Introduction to Text
Linguistics*, Longman,
                London

Bell, R. T. (1991)   *Translation and Translating:
Theory and Practice*, Longman,
New York

Bowen, J.C.E. (1973)   *Translation or Travesty*, Abbey
Press, Berkshire

Burgess, J. (1990)   *What We Listen to: Dialogue*,
Centre for English Language
Studies in Education, University of
Manchester, Manchester

Bygate, M. (1987)   *Speaking*, OUP, Oxford

Catford, J.C. (1965)   *A Linguistic Theory of Translation;*
                                  An essay in Applied Linguistics,
                                  OUP, London cited in Bassnet, S.
                                  (1991) *Translation Studies*,
                                  Routledge, London & New York
                                  (Revised Edition)

Chomsky, N. (1957)   *Syntactic Structures*, Mouton, The
Hague

Coombes, H. (1953)   *Literature and Criticism*, Penguin
Books

Darbyshire, A. A. (1971)   *A Grammar of Style*, Andre Deutch,
London

Eagleton. T. (1983)   *Literary Theory*, Blackwell, Oxford

Freeman, D. C. (1975)   "Style and Structure in Literature"
in *The New Style*,
                    Fowler, R. (Ed), Basil Blackwell, Oxford

Graves, R. & Shah. O. A. (1967) *The Rubaiyyat of Omar
Khayyam*, Cassell, London

Gray, M. (1984)   *A Dictionary of Literary Terms*,
Longman, York

Grice, H.P. (1975)   "Logic and Conversation" in Cole
                                  (Ed), *Syntax and Semantics:*
                                  Pragmatics, (1975), Academic
                                  Press, New York

Halliday, M & Hasan, R (1985) "Language, Context and Text:
Aspects of Language" in

A Social Semiotic Perspective,
OUP, Oxford

Halliday, M. (1985)   *An Introduction to Functional*
Grammar, Edward

Arnold, London

Hatim, B. & Mason, I. (1990) *The Translator as Communicator*,
Routledge,

New York

Haywood, J.A. & Nahmas, H.M. (1962) *A New Arabic Grammar*,
Percy Lund,

Humpheries

Leech, G. & Short, M. (1981)   *Style in Fiction*, Longman,
London

Lyons, J. (1981)   *Language and Linguistics: An*
Introduction, CUP,

Cambridge

Marsh, N. (1998)   *Analysing Texts: Virginia Woolf,*
the Novel, St Martins

Press, New York

McEldowney, P.L. (1990)   *Grammar and Communication in*
Learning A, MD339,

Unit 2, "Communicative Purposes",

University   of   Manchester,

Manchester

McEldowney, P.L. (1990a)   *Grammar and Communication in Learning B*, MD340,
    Unit 2, "Determiners and General Discourse Reference",

University of Manchester, Manchester

McEldowney, P.L. (1990b)   *Grammar and Communication in Learning B*, MD340,
        Unit 3, "Determiners and Specific

Discourse

        Reference," University of

Manchester, Manchester

McEldowney, P.L. (1992)   *Grammar and Communication in*

Learning B, MD340,

        Unit 7, "Epithets: Grammar and

Learning", University

        of Manchester

McEldowney, P.L. (1993)   *Grammar and Communication in*

Learning A, MD 339,

        "Learning Problems & Grammatical

Description",   University of Manchester, Manchester

McEldowney, P.L. (1994) *Tests in English Language Skills: Rationale: Part One:*

"Principles", CENTRA, Chorley

McEldowney, P.L. (1996/7) *Language and Learning,* Part One, "The Language", Oldham LEA, Oldham

McEldowney, P.L. (1996/7a) *Language and Learning,* Part Two, "An Integrated learning Cycle", Oldham LEA, Oldham

Milic, L.T. (1971) "Rhetorical Choice and Stylistic Options" in Chatman &

Seymour (Ed) (1971), *Literary Style: A Symposium,* Oxford, London

Muir, K. (1979) *Shakespeare's Sonnets*, George Allen & Unwin Ltd, London

Newmark, P. (1981) *Approaches to Translation,* Pergamon, Oxford

Newmark, P. (1987) "The Use of Systematic Linguistics in Translations Analysis" in Steele, R. & Threadgold T. (Eds), *Language Topics: Essays in Honour of Michael Halliday*, John Benjamin, Amsterdam & Philadelpia

Quirk, R. (1968) *The Use of English*, Longman, London

Recananti, F (1987) *Meaning & Force: The Pragmatics*

	of Performative Utterance, CUP, Cambridge
Saussure, F. D. (1959) trans. By Baskin,W.	*A Course in General Linguistics,*
	(1960), Peter Owen, London
Searle, J. (1969)	*Speech Acts*, Cambridge, London
Steiner, G. (1975) *and Translation*, OUP,	*After Babel: Aspects of Language*
	Oxford
Stubbs, M. (1983)	*Discourse Analysis: The Sociolinguistic Analysis of Natural Language*, OUP, Oxford
Van Dijk, T.A. (1972) London	*Text and Context*, Longman,
Vendler, H. (1997)	*The Art of Shakespeare's Sonnet*, Harvard University Press, Harvard

English Sources

Christie, A. (1991)	*A Problem at Pollensa Bay & Other Stories*, Fontana, London
Crane, R.S. (Ed) (1932) *1660 – 1800,* Harper &	*A Collection of English Poems:*
	Brothers, New York
Hamlyn (Pub.) (1985) Hamlyn Publishing	*Every Boy's New Handbook*, The
	Group Ltd, London

Hatim, B. (1994)   *English – Arabic – English*
                                     Translation: A Factual Text
                                     Linguistic Guide, The King Fahd
                                     School of Translation, Tangier

Holt, P. (2000)   "The Angel of the Veld, Emily
Hobhouse", *History for*
                     All, **Vol. 2, Issue 6. Dec/Jan IMP**

                                     ***Wildlife Explorer*, Pack 04,**
                                     International Masters Publishers
                                     Ltd, Italy

Joyce, J.   *Portrait of the Artist as a Young*
Man, Published, 1992,
                     Wordsworth Editions, London

Kenan, A. (1986)   *The Road to Ein Harood*, Alsaqi
Books, London

Kindersley (Pub.) (1991)   *Children's Illustrated*
Encyclopaedia, Dorling
                     Kindersley London

Mackean, D.G. (1973)   *Introduction to Biology*, John
Murray, London

Mansfield, K. (1922)   in Cumberlege, G. (1954),
                                     Katherine Mansfield: Selected
                                     Stories, OUP, Oxford

Ong, J. et al (1977)   "Love Beyond Death" in *Reading*
                                     and Understanding, Pan Pacific
                                     Book in association with Manhattan
                                     Press, Singapore

Payne, R. (1960)   *The White Rajahs of Sarawak,*
OUP, Singapore

Peres, S. (1995)   *Battling for Peace: Memoirs.*
Orion, Great Britain

Rushdie, S (1988)   *The Satanic Verses,* Viking,
London

Stannard, R (1996)   *Our Universe,* Kingfisher, New
York

Vordeman, C. (1997)   *How Mathematics Works,* Dorling
Kindersley, London

Woolf, V.   *To the Lighthouse,* Triad Grafton
Books, London

Arabic Sources

مصادر عربية:

إبراهيم زعرور:مكان ضيق...شديد الضيق، منشورات وزارة الثقافة، المملكة الأردنية الهاشمية، 1997 ،صفحة 11-12.

بدر توفيق: الترجمة الكاملة لسنوتات شكسبير (Material used in a coursework at Salford University)

سميرة ترمس: فن الطبخ والحلويات العربية، دار الهدى، بيروت-لبنان،1985، صفحة 126.

عبد الحميد جودة السحار: العرب في أوروبا-عبد الرحمن وطرف،مكتبة مصر،صفحة 7 (لا يوجد تاريخ نشر).

د. عمر محمد الأسعد (وآخرون): لغتنا العربية، وزارة التربية،عمان، 1996، صفحة

32.

لجنة تأليف: كتاب العلوم للصف الرابع الابتدائي، عمان مطبعة دار الكتب العلمية، 1995، صفحة 84.

لجنة تأليف: الجغرافيا للسنة السابعة، وزارة التربية الوطنية، المملكة المغربية، دار الثقافة للنشر، صفحة 74.

نقولا شاهين، د. يوسف دياب، أحمد الخطيب: الموسوعة العلمية الميسرة، مكتبة لبنان، 1982، صفحة 14 .

Author Index

Subject Index